Inside SCIENCE

Mental Illness Research

Other titles in the *Inside Science* series:

Inside SCIENCE

Mental Illness Research

Carla Mooney

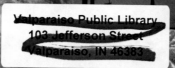

ReferencePoint
Press®

San Diego, CA

© 2012 ReferencePoint Press, Inc.
Printed in the United States

For more information, contact:
ReferencePoint Press, Inc.
PO Box 27779
San Diego, CA 92198
www. ReferencePointPress.com

LIBRARY OF CONGRESS CATALOGING-IN-PUBLICATION DATA

Mooney, Carla, 1970-
  Mental illness research / by Carla Mooney.
    p. cm. -- (Inside science series)
  Includes bibliographical references and index.
  ISBN-13: 978-1-60152-234-4 (hardback)
  ISBN-10: 1-60152-234-7 (hardback)
 1. Mental illness--Juvenile literature. I. Title.
  RC460.2.M66 2012
  362.196'890072--dc23
                                        2011036648

Contents

Foreword

I n 2008, when the Yale Project on Climate Change and the George Mason University Center for Climate Change Communication asked Americans, "Do you think that global warming is happening?" 71 percent of those polled—a significant majority—answered "yes." When the poll was repeated in 2010, only 57 percent of respondents said they believed that global warming was happening. Other recent polls have reported a similar shift in public opinion about climate change.

Although respected scientists and scientific organizations worldwide warn that a buildup of greenhouse gases, mainly caused by human activities, is bringing about potentially dangerous and long-term changes in Earth's climate, it appears that doubt is growing among the general public. What happened to bring about this change in attitude over such a short period of time? Climate change skeptics claim that scientists have greatly overstated the degree and the dangers of global warming. Others argue that powerful special interests are minimizing the problem for political gain. Unlike experiments conducted under strictly controlled conditions in a lab or petri dish, scientific theories, facts, and findings on such a critical topic as climate change are often subject to personal, political, and media bias—whether for good or for ill.

At its core, however, scientific research is not about politics or 30-second sound bites. Scientific research is about questions and measurable observations. Science is the process of discovery and the means for developing a better understanding of ourselves and the world around us. Science strives for facts and conclusions unencumbered by bias, distortion, and political sensibilities. Although sometimes the methods and motivations are flawed, science attempts to develop a body of knowledge that can guide decision makers, enhance daily life, and lay a foundation to aid future generations.

The relevance and the implications of scientific research are profound, as members of the National Academy of Sciences point out in the 2009 edition of *On Being a Scientist: A Guide to Responsible Conduct in Research:*

Some scientific results directly affect the health and well-being of individuals, as in the case of clinical trials or toxicological studies. Science also is used by policy makers and voters to make informed decisions on such pressing issues as climate change, stem cell research, and the mitigation of natural hazards. . . . And even when scientific results have no immediate applications—as when research reveals new information about the universe or the fundamental constituents of matter—new knowledge speaks to our sense of wonder and paves the way for future advances.

The *Inside Science* series provides students with a sense of the painstaking work that goes into scientific research—whether its focus is microscopic cells cultured in a lab or planets far beyond the solar system. Each book in the series examines how scientists work and where that work leads them. Sometimes, the results are positive. Such was the case for Edwin McClure, a once-active high school senior diagnosed with multiple sclerosis, a degenerative disease that leads to difficulties with coordination, speech, and mobility. Thanks to stem cell therapy, in 2009 a healthier McClure strode across a stage to accept his diploma from Virginia Commonwealth University. In some cases, cutting-edge experimental treatments fail with tragic results. This is what occurred in 1999 when 18-year-old Jesse Gelsinger, born with a rare liver disease, died four days after undergoing a newly developed gene therapy technique. Such failures may temporarily halt research, as happened in the Gelsinger case, to allow for investigation and revision. In this and other instances, however, research resumes, often with renewed determination to find answers and solve problems.

Through clear and vivid narrative, carefully selected anecdotes, and direct quotations each book in the *Inside Science* series reinforces the role of scientific research in advancing knowledge and creating a better world. By developing an understanding of science, the responsibilities of the scientist, and how scientific research affects society, today's students will be better prepared for the critical challenges that await them. As members of the National Academy of Sciences state: "The values on which science is based—including honesty, fairness, collegiality, and openness—serve as guides to action in everyday life as well as in research. These values have helped produce a scientific enterprise of unparalleled usefulness, productivity, and creativity. So long as these values are honored, science—and the society it serves—will prosper."

Important Events in Mental Illness Research

1883

German psychiatrist Eric Kraepelin, taking a more scientific approach to studying mental illness than his predecessors, distinguishes separate mental disorders.

1924

American psychologist Mary Cover Jones introduces a behavioral therapy approach to help children unlearn fears. Behavioral therapy would eventually be merged with cognitive therapy to form cognitive-behavioral therapy.

1935

The world's first modern frontal leukotomy (later known as lobotomy) is performed in a Lisbon hospital by Portuguese neurologist Antonio Egas Moniz. The procedure destroys brain tissue in an effort to alter behavior in a person with mental illness.

1915   **1925**   **1935**   **1945**

1841

Dorothea Dix begins a 40-year crusade to establish state hospitals for people with mental illness. Through her efforts to improve conditions for mentally ill jail inmates and others, Dix demonstrates that not all mental illnesses are incurable.

1937

Italian researchers Ugo Cerletti and Lucio Bini introduce electrically induced seizures to treat mental illness, the only form of electroconvulsive therapy accepted today.

1946

President Harry Truman signs the National Mental Health Act, calling for a National Institute of Mental Health to conduct research into mind, brain, and behavior and thereby reduce mental illness. NIMH is formally established on April 15, 1949.

1949

Australian researcher John Cade reports the benefits of lithium to treat 10 patients with mania.

1950
Chlorpromazine, the world's first antipsychotic drug used to treat schizophrenia, is first synthesized.

1963
The United States passes the Mental Retardation Facilities and Community Mental Health Centers Construction Act, which provides the first federal money for developing a network of community-based mental health services.

1957
Iproniazid, one of the first antidepressants, is synthesized. It was originally developed as a treatment for tuberculosis but became widely prescribed in the late 1950s to treat depression.

2011
Advanced brain imaging techniques are giving scientists an opportunity to study and identify specific circuits that are involved in mood disorders and study the effectiveness of medical and behavioral treatments.

1979
National Alliance for the Mentally Ill (NAMI) is founded to provide support, education, advocacy, and research services for people with serious psychiatric illnesses.

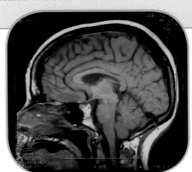

1950   **1960**   **1970**   **1980**   **1990**

1970
Lithium is approved by the FDA to treat mania.

1986
The National Alliance for Research on Schizophrenia and Depression is formed, becoming the largest nongovernment, donor-supported organization that distributes funds for brain disorder research.

1990
US president George H.W. Bush declares the decade starting in 1990 the Decade of the Brain.

1952
The American Psychiatric Association publishes the first *Diagnostic and Statistical Manual of Mental Disorders* (*DSM*), which is still used today by clinicians and researchers in the United States and around the world to diagnose and treat mental disorders.

1989
Clozapine is introduced. It is part of a new generation of antipsychotic drugs that prove to be more effective in treating schizophrenia with fewer side effects.

Changing Lives

I n the third grade, Brooke Katz began hearing voices. She quickly real- ized that other people could not hear the voices; they only spoke to her. The voices hissed at Katz that they were going to kill her, that they hated her, and that she should die. Katz remembers running from the classroom into the hall, closing her eyes, and curling into a ball on the floor. But no matter what she did, the voices followed her.

Soon, Katz was also seeing threatening figures. "I'd be sitting in class and look out the window and there would be these huge men, with guns and knives and they'd be staring at me and threatening me," she says. The voices in her head turned Katz's thoughts violent. "I stood in the shower, contemplating life and death. How would I kill myself?" she says. "I would look at someone and then they would get stuck in my head, and I would start violently torturing them inside my head, and I wouldn't hurt anyone, but they would be in my head, these violent thoughts."[1]

For years, Katz told no one about the voices that tortured her. By the time she was 17, she could no longer hide the stress of living with mental illness. One night, her parents rushed her to the emergency room. They were shocked when Katz was diagnosed with schizo-affective disorder, a mental illness that is characterized by recurring episodes of elevated or depressed mood that alternate with or occur together with distortions in perception. "As a mother, I can admit, I worried about everything. I worried about children doing drugs, and getting in with the wrong crowds and get- ting home late and driving after curfew. Every single thing I could possibly worry about, I did. It was never on my radar screen, to worry about mental illness,"[2] says Brooke's mother, Elsie Katz.

> **preemptive**
>
> A preventive measure.

To control her illness, Katz spent time in and out of hospitals and residential treatment centers for years. She tried more than 30 different medications and combinations. "I was so bad I had top doctors tell me I'll never get better. Very top doctors [said,] 'You'll be in institutions the rest of your life. You'll never graduate from school. You'll never have a family,'" says Katz.[3]

10

A Leading Cause of Disability

Mental illnesses like Katz's are serious and can be life-threatening. In the United States and Canada, mental health disorders are the leading cause of disability. They account for 25 percent of all years of life lost to disability and premature death. If mental illness is not treated, it can impact all areas of a person's life—impairing his or her ability to learn,

The 1990s, known as the Decade of the Brain, brought new insights into the workings of the brain. Ongoing scientific research promises a greater understanding of the relationship between the brain and mental illness. Pictured is a false-color MRI scan of a healthy human brain.

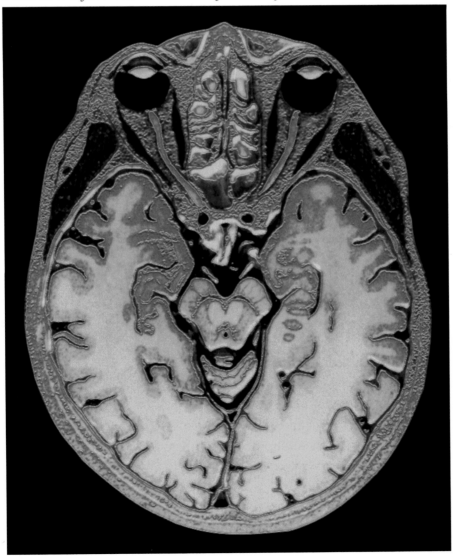

increasing the risk for other illnesses, making interpersonal relationships more difficult, and leading to problems at home and at work. In addition, untreated mental illness has been linked to suicide, which is the eleventh leading cause of death in the United States.

The National Institute of Mental Health (NIMH) is the country's scientific leader in mental illness research. Over the past decades, mental illness research has made rapid strides toward understanding the science behind mental illness and the medications to treat it. In the 1990s, known as the Decade of the Brain, research led to insights into the fundamental ways the brain functions and advanced methods for studying how the brain, behavior, and the environment interact and influence each other.

Changing Lives with Research

As mental illness research moves into the twenty-first century, researchers acknowledge that much work still has to be done. "For too many people with mental disorders even the best of current care is not good enough. . . . We must continue to discover the fundamental knowledge about brain and behavior and use such discoveries to develop better tools for diagnosis, preemptive interventions, more effective treatment and improved strategies for delivering services for those who provide direct mental care,"[4] says Thomas R. Insel, director of the NIMH.

For scientists, the desire to prevent suffering and premature death is often the driving force behind mental illness research. Daniel Weinberger, a senior investigator at the NIMH, became interested in mental illness, especially schizophrenia, because of the profound suffering associated with these diseases for both the patients

schizophrenia

A severe mental disorder that commonly includes symptoms such as hallucinations, paranoid or bizarre delusions, and disorganized speech and thinking.

and their families. "The purpose of research is to change the lives of sick people. So those are the things that stand there as the guiding beacon for why one does this,"[5] says Weinberger.

Because of the efforts of scientists like Weinberger, there is hope for people with mental illness. Ongoing research continues to yield new understanding, medications, and treatments for mental illnesses. These discoveries have helped Brooke Katz and others like her live with their disease. With regular therapy sessions and a new medication, her thoughts are clearer today than ever before. She has graduated college and works as a nurse and mental health educator. "It makes me feel hopeful, the research that is being done. We need research to figure out why does this happen to people and then when it does happen, what kind of early interventions can we do to stop things from progressing, to stop people from having to suffer for years and years and years like I suffered,"[6] she says.

What Is Mental Illness?

O n January 8, 2011, 22-year-old Jared Loughner unleashed a deadly shooting spree in the parking lot of a Tucson, Arizona, grocery store. Six people were killed and 14 others injured, including US representative Gabrielle Giffords. In the aftermath of the violent shooting, investigators searched for a reason why Loughner, a man who did not have a criminal record, would suddenly become deadly that winter morning.

In the weeks after the shooting, people close to Loughner said there were warning signs that he may have been suffering from an untreated mental illness—although few recognized these as signs of a serious problem until after the fact. For months before the shooting, Loughner exhibited disorganized thoughts and speech. According to classmates and instructors, he regularly made irrelevant and nonsense comments in his classes at Pima Community College. Friends said Loughner showed symptoms of psychosis and paranoia. Several classmates said that Loughner scared them. "What you see is a portrait of somebody with a major mental illness, of psychotic proportions, and I think it's probably likely that he suffers from schizophrenia,"[7] says Mark Kalish, a forensic therapist who was not involved in the case.

> ### psychosis
>
> A mental disorder characterized by symptoms such as delusions or hallucinations that indicate a person has impaired contact with reality.

Yet if Loughner did suffer from schizophrenia or another mental illness, doctors believe the illness may have prevented him from seeking treatment. "Most young people who develop a psychiatric illness—particularly a psychotic illness in which they've lost the ability to discern fantasy from reality—don't have a lot of insight into the fact that they are ill,"[8] says Ken Duckworth, a Harvard professor, psychiatrist and medical director of the National Alliance on Mental Illness (NAMI). In fact, Duckworth says that a recent NAMI survey found that schizophrenics suffer from symptoms for an average of nine years before they are diagnosed with the illness.

CHAPTER ONE

More than Feeling Sad

Mental illness is more than just feeling sad or blue for a few days or acting silly in front of friends. Mental illness is a serious health condition that changes the way a person thinks, feels, and behaves. It impairs a person's ability to function in everyday life. Like many diseases, mental illness can be mild or severe. Some people suffering from mental illness may not look outwardly sick. Others may appear confused, agitated, or withdrawn.

Jared Loughner (pictured) killed 6 people and wounded 14 others including US representative Gabrielle Giffords in January 2011. After the shootings, acquaintances described behavior that suggests that Loughner might have suffered from untreated mental illness.

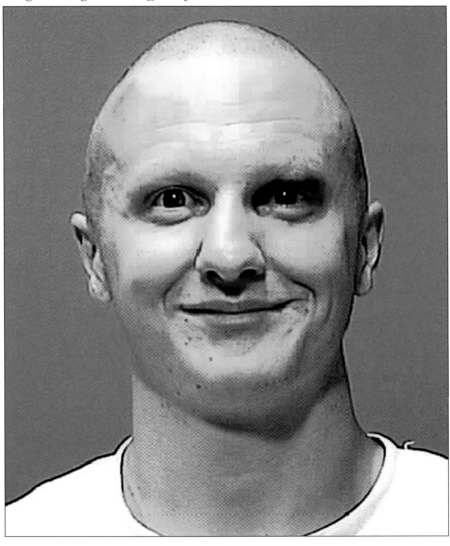

There are more than 200 forms of mental illness, including depression, schizophrenia, attention deficit hyperactivity disorder (ADHD), autism, Alzheimer's disease, and obsessive-compulsive disorder (OCD). Each illness affects a person's thoughts, feelings, and behaviors in unique ways. Affected people may have changes in mood, personality, and behavior. People suffering from depressive disorders often feel sad and hopeless. They might have difficulty concentrating or have thoughts of suicide. Schizophrenia can cause hallucinations and delusions. People with ADHD might have difficulty processing information as quickly and accurately as others, while people with autism spectrum disorders might have difficulty connecting or communicating with other people, or they might engage in repetitive behaviors.

Mental Illness in Adults

Many people think that mental illnesses are rare and will not happen to someone in their family. Actually, mental illnesses are common and widespread. According to the National Institutes of Health (NIH), approximately 26.2 percent of Americans or about one in four people over the age of eighteen has a diagnosable mental illness in any given year. In addition, four of the top ten leading causes of disability are mental illnesses—major depression, bipolar disorder, schizophrenia, and obsessive-compulsive disorder. In addition, many people suffer from more than one mental illness at a time. About 45 percent of people with a mental disorder meet the criteria for two or more disorders.

Mental illness is an equal-opportunity disease. It can strike people from any race, gender, nationality, or background. Shonda Schilling, wife of former Major League Baseball championship pitcher and six-time All Star Curt Schilling, seemed to have a picture-perfect life. A full-time mother and wife, she had four children, a comfortable lifestyle, and a famous husband. Behind closed doors, however, Shonda struggled with undiagnosed depression.

> It's hard to believe I was unaware of my depression. But, I hid it from everyone, including myself. I would crawl into bed when the kids went to school and sleep until 1:00 p.m. when I needed to get up to take care of them. I felt like I could fall asleep at any moment. I felt like I had worked for days and days and hadn't slept. The depression was big and affected how I felt in every way.[9]

Thomas R. Insel, Director of the National Institute of Mental Health

Since the fall of 2002, Thomas R. Insel has served as the director of the National Institute of Mental Health (NIMH). The NIMH leads the United States' research on mental disorders that affect millions of Americans. In this role, Insel manages a budget of more than $1.3 billion and is responsible for directing research efforts to understand mental illness better and how to effectively treat and prevent mental disorders.

After graduating from Boston University's Medical School, Insel began his career in mental illness in 1979, joining the NIMH. Over the next 15 years, he worked in several scientific research positions, conducting research in obsessive-compulsive disorder (OCD). He led some of the first treatment trials for OCD using the selective serotonin reuptake inhibitors (SSRI) class of medications.

In 1994 Insel left the NIMH to join Emory University in Atlanta as a professor of psychiatry. There, he was a founding director of the Center for Behavioral Neurosciences, one of the largest science and technology centers funded by the National Science Foundation. He was also the director of the Center for Autism Research. At Emory, Insel continued research he had started at the NIMH and studied the neurobiology of complex social behaviors in animals. In 2002, Insel returned to the NIMH with his appointment as Director.

In addition to his post at the NIMH, Insel serves on many academic, scientific, and professional committees and editorial boards. He has won numerous awards and has published hundreds of articles and papers and several books.

For Bud Clayman, mental illness sidetracked his dreams of becoming a journalist and filmmaker. In the 1980s he had a nervous breakdown and several episodes of severe depression. In addition to depression, he was later diagnosed with obsessive-compulsive disorder and Asperger's syndrome, a mild form of autism. Over the years, Clayman has dealt with unemployment and hospitalizations caused by his mental illnesses. Every day can be a challenge for Clayman where something as simple as riding the bus to work can cause stress. Asperger's makes it hard for him to read social clues and facial expressions from the people around him.

"With the Aspergers I am constantly worrying did I do the right thing, did I do that right, and that's a form of obsessing, and I'll think about my thoughts instead of just having the thoughts, so it becomes a whole cycle, and that is very nerve-wracking and irritating,"[10] he says.

Mental Illness in Children and Adolescents

Mental illness is not limited to adults; it can also affect children and adolescents. Approximately 12 million young people under age 18 have diagnosable mental disorders, or one in five children is affected by mental illness at any given time. According to the National Mental Health Association, as many as one out of 33 children may be depressed, with the rate rising to one out of eight in adolescents. For children with troubled backgrounds, the risk may be even higher. According to the National Institutes of Health, between 118,700 and 186,600 youths in the juvenile justice system have at least one mental illness. In addition, approximately 60 percent of teenagers in juvenile detention have behavioral, cognitive, or emotional problems stemming from mental illness.

Sixteen-year-old Nicole Cabezas showed signs of mental illness for years before being formally diagnosed with bipolar disorder. From the age of 14, she isolated herself in her bedroom, refused to socialize or do schoolwork, and thought about committing suicide. When the depression began to lift, Cabezas found herself in a state of high energy. Her thoughts raced, she spoke in fragments, and went without sleep for days. Her self-image was also impaired. "I was the center of the universe. I was the chosen one,"[11] she says. Finally, when Cabezas began to have delusions and believed that she had telekinetic powers, her mother took her to the emergency room. After a two-week inpatient hospital stay, Cabezas was released with a therapy plan and a combination of medications. Six months later, doctors confirmed a diagnosis of bipolar disorder.

Causes of Mental Illness

Scientists do not have a complete understanding of what causes mental illness. The complexity of the brain along with the varied effects that mental illnesses can have on thoughts, feelings, and behaviors makes it a challenge to study. Scientists in the fields of neuroscience, psychiatry, and psychology are investigating how brain biology and behavior affect each other. Most scientists believe that a combination of biological, genetic, environmental, and social factors interact to influence whether someone becomes mentally ill. Because each person reacts differently to these factors, predicting who will develop a mental illness is often difficult.

Most scientists believe that chemical imbalances in the brain are connected to mental illness. Chemicals called neurotransmitters affect how a person thinks, feels, and acts. Neurotransmitters carry messages from the brain to different parts of the body. In people with mental illness, these chemicals can get out of balance, and the messages can be lost or distorted. Scientists have found that the neurotransmitter serotonin is lower in patients with depression than patients who do not have the mood disorder. Other neurotransmitters such as dopamine, glutamate, and norepinephrine have been found to be out of balance in patients with schizophrenia. Researchers have also found that some people with mental illness

neurotransmitters

Chemical substances such as serotonin or dopamine that transmit nerve impulses across a synapse or gap to another nerve, muscle, or gland.

have abnormal levels of hormones in their blood. For example, about 50 percent of people with clinical depression have an excess of cortisol, a hormone that helps the body regulate its reaction to stress, in their blood.

A person's genes may also be a factor in whether the person develops a mental illness. Research has shown that people from families with a history of mental illness have a greater risk of developing a mental illness. Mental illnesses with the strongest genetic component include autism, bipolar disorder, schizophrenia, and ADHD. Fifty percent of people with bipolar disorder have a parent with a history of clinical depression. Children with ADHD are much more likely to have a sibling or parent with ADHD. In addition, ADHD is significantly more likely to appear in identical twins rather than in fraternal twins. Although these findings suggest a genetic link to mental illness, scientists are still figuring out which genes are involved and how they influence mental illness. "We've known that genes play a significant role in the risk of these disorders. But until very recently, it's been difficult to impossible to identify genes that lead to these illnesses,"[12] says Jordan Smoller, director of the Psychiatric Genetics Program in Mood and Anxiety Disorders at Massachusetts General Hospital.

Environmental factors can also increase the risk of developing a mental illness. Studies of identical twins have found that if one twin develops schizophrenia, the other will develop it less than 50 percent of the time. Because the twins have the same genetic makeup, these results suggest that environmental influences are involved. Scientists believe environmental triggers such as head injuries, poor nutrition, and exposure to toxins including lead and tobacco smoke can increase a person's risk of developing a mental illness. In addition, social factors can increase the risk, particularly for children. Stressful events such as the death of a loved one, abuse, job loss, or end of a relationship may make a person more vulnerable to mental illness.

Not everyone experiencing stress or even trauma develops a mental illness. The exact same event may harm one person's mental health but not another's. To understand better the role environment plays in mental illness, scientists are pursuing a line of research to understand how early-life events might influence brain development and adult behavior.

Warning Signs

Mental disorders are often hard to detect because the behaviors they cause vary widely from person to person. "They're defined mainly by thoughts, behaviors, and feelings. We don't have biological measures on which to rest our diagnoses,"[13] says Ezra Susser, a psychiatrist and department chair in epidemiology at the Columbia University Mailman School of Public Health.

While each mental illness has its own characteristic symptoms, several general warning signs could indicate a possible disorder. Personality changes, excessive anxieties, prolonged depression or apathy, strange or grand ideas, and extreme mood swings are warning signs for mental illness. In addition, a person struggling with a mental disorder may be unable to cope with daily activities and problems or may experience changes in eating or sleeping patterns. Looking for a way to cope, a person with a mental illness may turn to drugs or alcohol. Other times they may seem excessively angry and appear hostile and violent. In some cases, people suffering from mental illness lose hope and think or talk about suicide as a way to escape their disorder.

apathy

A lack of feeling or emotion, interest, or concern.

Eighteen-year-old David started behaving strangely a few weeks after beginning his freshman year of college. When he surprised his mother with an unplanned 3 a.m. visit home, she noticed immediately that something was wrong. "David was acting weird. He was spacing out, he was very disheveled, saying things that weren't making sense at all. He cried a lot. He was listening to one CD on repeat. I kept asking what went through his mind, but he wouldn't answer,"[14] says his mother. Recognizing her son's odd behavior as a warning sign, David's mother took him to the doctor, who determined that David could be in the early stages of a psychotic episode.

Although identifying the warning signs of mental illness may be difficult, experts say that early identification and treatment may make a significant difference in a patient's outcome. "Catching the illness as early as possible means that you probably have an illness that is not as severe, [for which] interventions work better,"[15] says Oliver Freudenreich, a psychiatrist at Massachussetts General Hospital.

Diagnosing Mental Illness

If a person displays any warning signs for mental illness, he or she should be evaluated by a qualified professional who has expertise in mental illnesses. Mental health professionals include psychiatrists, psychologists, psychiatric nurses, social workers, and mental health counselors. In some cases, a mental health professional will refer a patient to a psychiatrist, who can prescribe medication.

Unlike some diseases, mental illness is not diagnosed with a blood test or X-ray. Instead, mental health professionals evaluate a patient's symptoms, mental state, and physical condition. The American Psychiatric Association publishes a guide, the *Diagnostic Statistical Manual of Mental Disorders (DSM-IV)*, that lists criteria for each recognized mental illness. Mental health professionals use this guide to evaluate patients.

At the first appointment, the mental health expert will usually ask the patient questions in order to evaluate his or her condition. Special questionnaires called mental health inventories record the person's feelings, physical symptoms, and daily experiences and can help with diagnosis. The professional will determine what symptoms the patient has, how severe they are, how long the symptoms have been experienced, and how the patient's life is affected by the symptoms. The mental health expert may gather information from family members about the patient, to help with diagnosis. During the evaluation, the mental health professional will conduct a physical exam to look for any medications, illnesses, or physical conditions that may be causing symptoms. Some types of strokes, thyroid disorders, and contraceptives can cause the same symptoms as a mental illness. If the mental health professional determines that the patient has a mental illness, he or she will work with the patient to develop an appropriate treatment plan.

Treating Mental Illness

Although most mental illnesses cannot be cured, they can usually be treated effectively. The right treatment can minimize symptoms and allow the patient to function at work, school, and in social environments. With psychotherapy, medication, or a combination treatment, most people can manage their mental illness and lead a productive life. According to the NIH, between 70 and 90 percent of patients have significant reduction of symptoms and an improved quality of life when treated with a combination of medication and psychotherapy.

psychotherapy

The treatment of mental or emotional disorders by psychological means and involving a trained psychiatrist or psychologist.

Treatments for mental illness may involve some type of psychotherapy, also known as talk therapy. Talk therapy can be individual, group, or family sessions. During a therapy session, a person talks with a mental health expert about his or her feelings and problems. Talking through these issues can help the person learn to recognize unhealthy thoughts and behaviors and to replace them with helpful ones. One of the most common types of talk therapy is cognitive-behavioral therapy (CBT), by which the patient learns techniques to change negative thoughts and behaviors into positive thinking.

Medications are also used to treat the symptoms of mental illnesses such as schizophrenia, depression, bipolar disorder, anxiety disorders, and ADHD. Medication cannot cure a patient, but it can help a person with a mental illness feel and function better in daily life. For some patients, medication plus psychotherapy is an effective combination.

synapses

Extremely small gaps between nerve cells where neurotransmitters travel.

Doctors frequently prescribe antipsychotic medications for schizophrenia patients. The majority of antipsychotics work by blocking the absorption of dopamine, a chemical that occurs naturally in the brain. Dopamine is one of the brain's messengers that transmit messages across the gaps or synapses of nerve cells. When dopamine levels are too

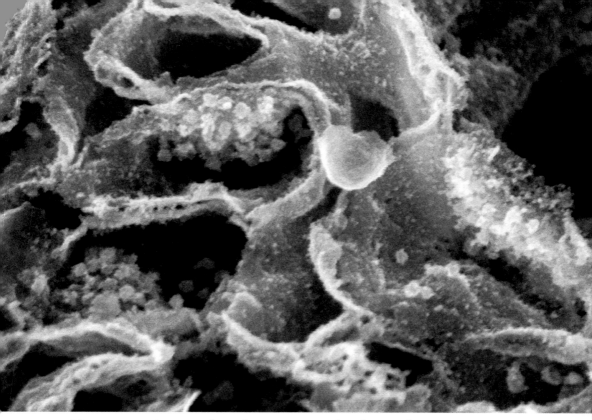

Neurotransmitters such as dopamine are the chemical messengers of the brain. They transmit messages across the gaps, or synapses, of nerve cells (shown here in a colored scanning electron micrograph). When an electrical signal reaches a synapse it triggers the release of neurotransmitters from vesicles (bright blue).

high, the brain can speed up nerve impulses, sometimes causing hallucinations, delusions, and thought disorders. When antipsychotic medications block dopamine absorption, they reduce the severity of symptoms.

Antidepressant medications are widely used to treat depression. These medications affect how neurotransmitters function and control mood. Several types of antidepressant medications treat depressive disorders, including selective serotonin reuptake inhibitors (SSRIs), tricyclics, and monoamine oxidase inhibitors (MAOIs). Bipolar patients may take mood stabilizers such as lithium to help even out dramatic mood swings.

Sometimes a patient can be most effectively treated in the hospital. This occurs most often when a person displays suicidal or life-threatening behavior. For those who are severely depressed, suicidal, or experiencing severe mania, doctors may consider electroconvulsive therapy (ECT) in which short electrical pulses trigger a seizure in the brain.

Sheldon Hill of Wayne, Michigan, experienced symptoms of bipolar disorder for many years. Finally in 2006, a girlfriend convinced him that his emotional outbursts were a sign of mental illness and that he should seek help. Therapy and medication helped Hill cope with his disorder. "I know now that it's like any other illness, heart disease or diabetes. You can manage it, and managing the disease allows me to function as well as any other individual."[16] says Hill.

Consequences of Not Treating Mental Illness

Yet despite the effectiveness of mental illness treatment, many people do not seek treatment. In 2008 a survey by the Substance Abuse and Mental Health Services Administration found that only approximately 59 percent of adults in the United States with a serious mental illness received treatment for their mental health problem. In addition, many people discontinue treatment too early because they do not like their medication's side effects or have started feeling better.

Not treating mental illness or not treating it effectively can have significant consequences. Researchers say that untreated mental illness can lead to more frequent and more severe episodes of the illness. Delaying treatment can lead to more treatment-resistant disorders. In addition, for children and teens, untreated mental illnesses can lead to failure in school, teenage pregnancy, problems at work and at home, and violence. Experts also say that treating these cases could prevent the illness from becoming more severe. "The pattern appears to be that the earlier in life the disorder begins, the slower an individual is to seek therapy, and the more persistent the illness. It's unfortunate that those who most need treatment are the least likely to get it,"[17] says Ronald C. Kessler, a professor of health care policy at Harvard Medical School.

Unpleasant side effects, financial costs, and social stigma are all reasons why people stop treatment or do not seek treatment for mental illness. According to clinical psychologist Hector Gonzales, the stigma around mental illness rises from a lack of understanding and knowledge about these disorders. "Some people don't see it as a medical disorder. There's this whole notion that you should be able to snap out of it or pull yourself up by your bootstraps,"[18] says Gonzales.

The Need for Mental Illness Research

Although treatments for mental illness are effective for some people, many more continue to suffer from a variety of mental disorders. Recog-

Mental Illness and Substance Abuse

People with some mental illnesses are more likely to abuse alcohol, drugs, or cigarettes. Many patients with mood disorders find they cannot cope with their feelings of sadness and depression. As a result, they turn to alcohol, drugs, or cigarettes to change how they feel. People with bipolar disorder in a manic phase may use drugs and alcohol to enhance their high. Schizophrenia patients may use drugs, cigarettes, or alcohol to escape hallucinations or delusions. A study published in the January 2008 issue of the *Archives of General Psychiatry* showed that people with mood disorders, particularly mania and bipolar disorder, had a high risk of developing a substance abuse problem. Researchers believe that earlier detection of mental illness could help prevent subsequent substance abuse problems.

Using drugs and alcohol to numb feelings may work in the short term, but substance abuse makes a person feel worse over time. Substance abuse may make it less likely that a patient will follow his or her treatment plan. In addition, it may interfere with mental illness medication. For schizophrenic patients, stimulants such as amphetamines or cocaine can cause a worsening of symptoms. In addition, cigarette smoking has been found to interfere with antipsychotic medications, leading patients to need higher doses.

Substance abuse can also lead to violence in mental illness patients. A 2009 study by researchers at the University of Oxford in England concluded that schizophrenia patients who also had a substance abuse problem were significantly more likely to commit a violent crime.

nizing the need for better treatments and greater understanding of mental illness, many doctors and scientists are working to improve the outcomes for treatment and recovery. "Many investigators, including myself are trying to shed light on the brain changes that set the stage for the onset of mental illnesses in late adolescence and early adulthood,"[19] says Elaine Walker, professor of psychology at Emory University and neuroscience editor of *Psychological Science in the Public Interest*.

Yet understanding the biological basis of mental illness is challenging. Symptoms vary among patients. Moreover, although many mental illnesses have been linked to genes, researchers have had difficulty in identifying more than a very small piece of a person's DNA that explains his or her risk of mental illness. Says Mortimer Mishkin, a researcher at the NIH,

> There is no more complex piece of matter in the universe than the human brain, and so the complexity is a huge challenge. Each brain area is important for a different kind of behavioral or mental function, yet no area is an island. Every area is part of a circuit. So we've been identifying pathways and trying to figure out how they work. As we're able to learn more about how the brain works and how to fix it, millions of people are going to benefit, and through that process understanding will develop about the role of science in having made all of that possible.[20]

Looking Deep Inside the Brain

I n 2009 a large brain-imaging study at Columbia University Medical Center and the New York State Psychiatric Institute found that people with at least one parent or grandparent diagnosed with depression had a 28 percent thinning of the brain's right cortex as compared with study participants with no such family history. In addition, the study found that subjects who had additional brain thinning on the left cortex went on to develop depression. "Our findings suggest rather strongly that if you have thinning in the right hemisphere of the brain, you may be predisposed to depression and may also have some cognitive and inattention issues. The more thinning you have, the greater the cognitive problems. If you have additional thinning in the same region of the left hemisphere that seems to tip you over from having a vulnerability to developing symptoms of an overt illness,"[21] says Bradley S. Peterson, a professor of psychiatry at Columbia College of Physicians and Surgeons.

cortex

The outer or superficial layer of an organ such as the brain.

Biological Basis for Mental Illness

For much of the twentieth century, the study of mental illness ignored how the brain functioned. Doctors believed mental illness was all in a patient's mind, a purely psychological process. They concentrated on psychological therapies, such as talk therapy, to treat mental disorders.

As the Columbia brain imaging study shows, however, researchers have realized that mental illness may have a biological basis, as do many other diseases. Modern brain imaging technologies are revealing that in many mental illnesses, the brain circuits and structures responsible for the regulation of moods, thinking, sleep, appetite, and behavior fail to function properly. For example, researchers now know that autism is caused by an abnormality in the connections between brain neurons.

CHAPTER TWO

Predisposed to Depression

A large brain-imaging study found that thinning in the right cerebral cortex, might make a person more susceptible to depression. The cerebral cortex is involved with reasoning, planning, and mood. Thinning in this region might affect the ability to process emotional stimuli, predisposing a person to anxiety and depression. This illustration shows a side view of the hemispheres of the brain. Blue and pink represent thinning, especially pronounced in the right hemisphere. Areas that are green, most prominent in the left hemisphere, signify little thinning. The pattern seen in the right hemisphere is consistent with a person who has a family history of depression.

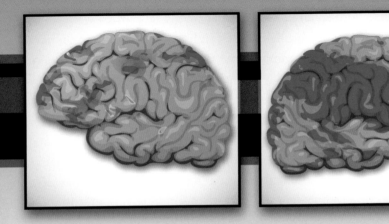

Source: Roni Caryn Rabin, "Study Links Depression to Thinning of Brain's Cortex," *New York Times*, March 24, 2009.

Recognizing that mental illness may have a physical cause, scientists want to learn more about the structural and chemical changes in the brain when a person has a mental illness. If they can figure out what happens in the brain, they may be able to develop better treatments or find cures.

Basics of Brain Function

Understanding how the brain functions normally is an important step for researchers studying the brain's changes during mental illness. The brain is a complex organ. It controls a person's memory, senses, and emotions. It also controls body processes such as movement and breathing.

The brain contains billions of nerve cells called neurons. Neurons are the basic unit of the brain. They communicate through electrical signals. Chemicals called neurotransmitters carry electrical messages from neuron to neuron. The brain and the nervous system use several types of neurotransmitter, including serotonin, dopamine, and norepinephrine. Each has a specific distribution and function in the brain. Neurotransmitters affect how a person thinks, feels, and acts. They carry messages from the brain to different parts of the body. For example, when a person puts his or her hand near something hot, the receptors on the hand send a message via neurons to the brain. In response, the brain sends a message back to the arm muscles to move the hand away from the heat.

Biological Basis of Mental Illness

Researchers studying mental illness believe that an imbalance of neurotransmitter chemicals in the brain may be a factor in many mental illnesses. If neurotransmitters are out of balance, the brain's messages can be lost or distorted, leading to the symptoms of mental illness. For example, studies have found that the level of serotonin is lower in people with depression. Some studies suggest that decreased serotonin levels may cause sleep disturbances, irritability, and anxiety. This finding led to the development of medications that increase serotonin in the patient's brain. Scientists also believe that disruptions in the neurotransmitters dopamine, glutamate, and norepinephrine may be a factor in schizophrenia.

cognitive

Having to do with the mental processes of perception, memory, judgment, and reasoning.

In addition to studying neurotransmitters, researchers are also investigating the ways that hormones affect mental disorders. Hormones are chemicals that help the body's organs function. For example, the body makes the hormone cortisol in response to stress, fear, or anger. In a typical person, cortisol levels peak in the morning, then taper off throughout the day. In people with depression, cortisol levels remain high throughout the day. High levels of cortisol have also been found in people with bipolar disorder. In women, scientists are also studying the effect that cyclical changes in hormones such as estrogen have on brain chemistry and mental disorders. In addition, abnormal thyroid gland function has been linked to bipolar disorder.

Another area of the brain that may influence mental disorders is the limbic system. Within the limbic system, a small structure called the hypothalamus regulates body temperature, sleep, appetite, sexual drive, stress reaction, and other activities. The hypothalamus also works with the adrenal glands to produce adrenaline. If the hypothalamus malfunctions, too much or too little adrenaline may be produced. With too much adrenaline, a person may experience mania. With too little adrenaline, he or she may fall into a depression. In addition, the hypothalamus also regulates the pituitary gland, which controls key hormones that may be involved with mental illness. Other structures in the limbic system such as the amygdala and the hippocampus affect emotions and judgment. Improper functioning of these areas may affect a person's mood and behavior.

amygdala

A structure in the brain's limbic system that is linked to emotions and aggression.

Researchers believe that variations in the size or shape of different parts of the brain may be factors in determining who develops a mental illness. Brain imaging shows that the brains of people with mental illness look different from the brains of those without these disorders. In particular, the parts of the brain that regulate mood, thinking, sleep, appetite, and behavior appear to function improperly.

Studying the Brain

To learn more about the chemical and structural changes that occur in the brain during mental illness, researchers called neuroscientists study the brain. If they can understand what happens in the brain, they can use that knowledge to develop better treatments or find cures for mental illness.

To understand how mental illness affects the brain, scientists try to visualize the changes in the brain. Visual images help them learn more about variations in brain activity or structure during mental illness. Historically, scientists could only examine the brains of patients who had already died. They were unable to see how a living brain worked and processed information. Today, however, new imaging procedures enable scientists to study the brain in living animals and humans. "Neuroimaging has opened up the black box of the brain so that mental disorders can, for the first time, be studied as abnormalities in the connections

Hormones such as adrenaline interact with neurotransmitters and other brain chemicals to influence overall health and well-being. Too much adrenaline can lead to mania; too little can lead to depression. A polarized light micrograph shows crystals of adrenaline.

between distant areas of the brain or in some cases, problems in the co-ordination of the brain areas whose activity is normally synchronized,"[22] says Thomas R. Insel.

Magnetic Resonance Imaging

Scientists use a variety of imaging techniques to study brain structure and function. One common way to study brain structure is through magnetic resonance imaging (MRI). An MRI uses strong magnets to create a snapshot of the brain's structures. The image shows bone, tissue, and blood vessels. MRIs will also reveal whether a patient has a brain tumor, infection, damage to the brain, or bleeding in the brain. Neuroscientists who are studying mental illness use MRIs to look for structural changes in the brains of mental illness patients. For example, MRI studies have shown that the ventricles or spaces within the brain are larger in schizophrenia patients than in healthy people. They have also shown that schizophrenia is related to structural deformities of the hippocampus, a part of the brain that is involved in memory forming, organizing, and storing.

> **neuroimaging**
>
> The use of various techniques to image the structure and function of the brain.

In 2010 researchers from the University of Edinburgh in Scotland announced that a new study might help predict the onset of schizophrenia. In the study, the research team examined brain scans of 146 young adults with a family history of schizophrenia, but who had not yet experienced any symptoms of the illness themselves. They compared the brain scans to scans of 36 people who were not at high risk for schizophrenia. Researchers repeated the brain scans on study participants every 18 months for a 10-year period. They noticed that in healthy people, the brain began to shrink slowly in early adulthood. For patients who would later develop schizophrenia, the brain shrank at an accelerated rate, before they became ill.

Researchers hope that this study will lead to doctors using structural brain scans to identify accelerated brain shrinkage in people at high risk for schizophrenia. They could diagnose schizophrenia and start treatment earlier, potentially improving a patient's quality of life. "This study represents the culmination of more than 10-years of work and is a significant step to understanding the origins of schizophrenia years before the onset of disability and medical treatment,"[23] says the study's lead author, Andrew McIntosh of the Division of Psychiatry at the University of Edinburgh.

Functional Imaging

While structural imaging shows the size and position of the brain's sections, functional imaging shows the activity and chemistry in the live brain. Functional imaging measures the rate of blood flow in the brain,

Studying a "Brainbow"

New neuroimaging techniques will help scientists understand how malfunctions of brain circuits affect mental illness by providing detailed images of brain activity and structures. One technique uses voltage-sensitive dye and is being tested in mice. Scientists have genetically engineered mice so that their neurons fluoresce in multiple colors when they fire. Each neuron in the mouse brain is stained with one of about a hundred different colors. When the neurons fire, the colors can be seen by fluorescent microscopy in a beautiful rainbow, or "brainbow," image.

The brainbow technique allows scientists to better study and map neural circuits because it allows them to easily distinguish neurons located next to each other. The multicolored images show scientists where and how neurons connect to each other. As the mouse grows and ages, scientists can study how the neural connections change. This way of looking at the brain may help scientists better understand what happens when brain circuits malfunction.

chemical activity, and electrical impulses in the brain of a live patient while he or she performs certain tasks.

One of the most common types of functional brain imaging is positron emission tomography (PET). In a PET scan, doctors inject small amounts of radioactive material into a patient's body. The material gives off gamma rays that are detected by a special gamma camera. The camera produces images that show the structure and function of internal organs, such as the brain. Computers reconstruct the images from a PET scan in two or three dimensions for scientists to review and analyze. Scientists use PET to measure changes in activity in the brains of people with mental illness and show where neurons are most active. They also use PET to measure how the brain activity changes or responds to mental illness treatment.

At the New York State Psychiatric Institute (NYSPI), researchers are using PET scans to study depression in patients. The scans have shown that patients with depression and bipolar disorder have abnormalities in the brain's neurotransmitter systems. Says John Mann, chief of the NYSPI Department of Neuroscience:

For years people have said that depression or mood disorders are a chemical imbalance in the brain. Now we have a large imaging center here on the medical campus and we're actually able to image brain neurotransmitter systems in patients. Now we've shown unequivocal evidence of neurotransmitter abnormalities in bipolar disorder and in major depression, and we've shown how these abnormalities can have an impact on the probability of patients responding to different types of treatment.[24]

Mann also hopes that current PET scan research will lead to better treatment for patients with depression and bipolar disorder. Currently, prescribing medication for depression patients is hit or miss, with doctors trying different medications and combinations until they find something that works. Mann believes that PET scans might help doctors predict the results of specific antidepressants, which could greatly improve treatment. He has obtained funding to study this approach further. A positive outcome in these studies "will change the treatment approach in the sense that patients would come in, see a physician, have a scan, and depending on results of the scan, the doctor can see which treatment they will be started out on,"[25] says Mann.

Studying the Living Brain

In addition to PET scans, scientists also use other techniques to study the function of the living brain. These techniques include single photon emission computer tomography (SPECT), functional magnetic resonance imaging (fMRI), and electroencephalography (EEG). Because each provides a different type of information about the brain's function, scientists will often use several of these techniques in their research.

At the University of Illinois at Chicago (UIC), researchers used brain imaging to study the effects of emotion in the brains of children with either pediatric bipolar disorder (PBD) or attention deficit hyperactivity disorder (ADHD). Both PBD and ADHD often result in impulsivity, irritability, and attention problems in patients. In the study, researchers used fMRI to examine the brain activity of children as they performed a working memory task while viewing faces with

electroencephalography

The measuring and recording of electrical activity in the brain.

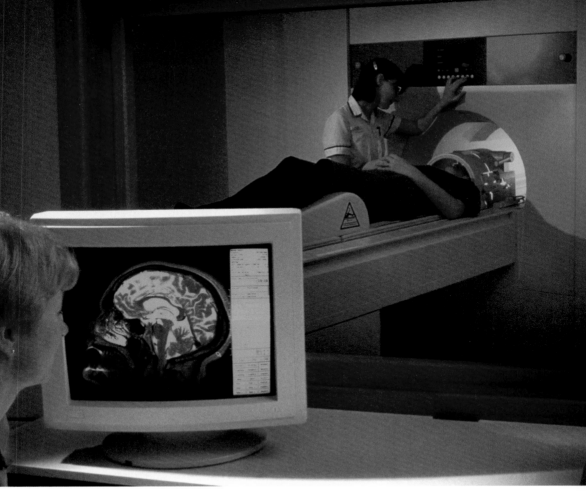

Scientists use a variety of imaging techniques to study the brain. Magnetic resonance imaging, or MRI, allows scientists to look for structural changes in the brains of people with mental illness. Here a woman undergoes an MRI. The digitized scan appears on a computer (left).

different emotions, such as happy, angry, or neutral. "It's a simple yet elegant working memory test that tells us a lot about how their brain remembers stimuli like faces or objects. We also added in an emotional component—because both disorders show emotional deficits—to study how their working memory is affected by emotional challenge,"[26] says Alessandra Passarotti, assistant professor of psychiatry at UIC and lead author of the study.

The researchers found that both disorders showed dysfunction in the brain's prefrontal cortex region. They also discovered differences in the dysfunction between the two groups of patients. While the ADHD group had greater dysfunction in working memory circuits in the brain, the bipolar group had more deficits in parts of the brain involved in emotion processing and regulation. "Our hope is that by better differentiating between these two severe developmental illnesses, we can help develop more accurate diagnoses and more targeted treatments for PBD and ADHD,"[27] says Passarotti.

Using Brain Scans to Study Depression

Neuroscience has led to rapid progress in understanding the biological basis of depression. Major depressive disorder, commonly known as depression, affects 16 percent of all Americans. It is the leading cause of medical disability for people between the ages of 15 and 44 worldwide. Depression symptoms include a profound sense of despair and a variety of physical symptoms, including sleep disturbances, appetite changes, and fatigue. It sometimes also disrupts the immune system and several hormonal systems.

Working in brain research, neurologist Helen Mayberg at Emory University made a discovery about depression with the help of brain imaging. Mayberg already knew that the brains of depressed patients looked different from those of healthy patients. However, there appeared to be no consistent pattern among the depressed brains. While studying brain scans of patients who had recovered from depression, she noticed that a tiny region of the brain called area 25 showed a consistent decrease in activity where activity had previously been elevated. Looking closely at patients' various imaging studies, Mayberg realized that turning down the brain activity in area 25 might be a key component of successfully treating depression. Mayberg knew that area 25 was located at a critical intersection of the brain. It had important connections to other areas of the brain that controlled mood, sleep, motivation, and drive. "This brain area is like it's at the core of all things. It's sitting in a place that when it goes wrong, havoc is wreaked,"[28] says Mayberg.

Further studying the brain scans, Mayberg realized that as the area 25 activity decreased, activity in the patient's frontal cortex increased. Previous studies had shown that depression patients often showed a decrease in activity in the frontal cortex, where the brain's command center is located. Mayberg suspected that the changing activity in the two areas was linked. To test her theory, she conducted a simple experiment. She asked healthy people to think sad thoughts while she scanned their brains. The scans revealed that area 25 became overactive while the frontal cortex

Brain Activity in Post-Traumatic Stress Disorder

In 2010 researchers from the University of Minnesota and the Minneapolis VA Medical Center announced that they had found differences in brain activity between people with post-traumatic stress disorder (PTSD) and healthy people. PTSD is an anxiety disorder that can occur after a person experiences a traumatic event that usually includes the threat of death or injury. It can cause flashbacks, nightmares, anger, or edginess.

In the Minnesota study, researchers scanned the brains of study participants, looking for a signal that might help identify PTSD patients from healthy volunteers. They used a highly sensitive magnetoencephalography (MEG) device, which measured the magnetic fields produced by electrical activity in the brain. Study participants wore a helmet with 248 noninvasive sensors spread around the head. Each participant was given a simple fixation task to engage his or her brain in a stable condition. Scientists mapped the patterns of electrical activity inside the skull. Using MEG, the Minnesota researchers found distinctive brain patterns in more than 97 percent of the participants who had been diagnosed with PTSD.

Researchers are now looking to confirm the study's finding with a larger study group. They hope their findings will one day help diagnose and monitor the effectiveness of treatments for PTSD patients.

activity slowed down, supporting the connection she suspected. According to Mayberg, healthy people can quickly recover from being sad, but a possible circuitry failure in depressed patients prevented them from doing the same.

Because of this study and others, neuroscientists believe depression is a brain circuitry disorder. Abnormal activity in area 25 may disrupt the brain's connected network. Disruptions may explain depressed patients' changes in appetite, sleep patterns, and energy levels. Disruptions to other areas that control anxiety, mood, memory processing, attention, and self-esteem are also affected. "A dysfunctional area 25 might therefore fail to coordinate the activity of these other centers so that information processing is biased, leading to distorted assessments of the internal and external world,"[29] says Insel.

Human Connectome Project

Despite the progress that has been made in brain research, scientists believe there is much more to learn. "It's like there's a continent there, and we are nibbling along the shores,"[30] says Van Wedeen, a physicist and radiologist at the Martinos Center for Biomedical Imaging at Massachusetts General Hospital. Wedeen is helping to lead an effort to develop a superscanner that can provide new insight into the brain.

Focusing on learning more about the brain, the NIH announced in 2009 that it was launching a massive project to create the first complete map of the complex circuitry of the healthy adult human brain. Over a five-year period, the Human Connectome Project will use innovative brain imaging technologies to collect data from hundreds of participants. Researchers hope that the project will give investigators insight on how brain connections support brain function and will open up new areas of brain study. "Neuroscientists have only a piecemeal understanding of brain connectivity. If we knew more about the connections within the brain—and especially their susceptibility to change—we would know more about brain dysfunction in aging, mental health disorders, addiction and neurological disease,"[31] says Story Landis, director of the National Institute of Neurological Disorders and Stroke.

Eventually, the Human Connectome Project plans to make comparisons of brains of healthy people with those of people with psychiatric diseases and developmental disorders. They hope to understand better how the differences in brain wiring and connections might affect behavior or disease. "Right now in the human brain . . . we have very little information about connectivity. People have had hypotheses for this for a long time, but we haven't had the data to really work on it. Schizophrenia is thought by some people to be disrupted connectivity; autism is increasingly thought of as perhaps aberrant connectivity. . . . What we're looking to do with the connectome project is fill in this crucial, but missing, class of data,"[32] says Michael Huerta, director of the National Institutes of Health Connectome Initiative.

Building a Better Picture of the Brain

As researchers learn more about the brain and how certain structures or functions may contribute to mental illness, they are building a better picture of how to predict which people are at a greater risk of developing a mental disorder. Scientists hope that as brain research reveals the brain areas and circuits that control thought and emotion, they can also learn how genetics, experiences, and environment affect the brain. This information might enable doctors to do a better job of preventing, diagnosing, and treating mental illness. "Today's developing science-based understanding of mental illness very likely will revolutionize prevention and treatment and bring real and lasting relief to millions of people worldwide,"[33] says Insel.

At the same time, as researchers dig deep into the brain to study how its structure and function affect mental illness, they recognize that the underlying causes of circuit malfunctions is a separate area of study. In some cases, gene mutations may lead to brain changes. In other cases, environmental sources and experiences may interact with genes to cause the brain changes linked to mental illness. In any case, the answer is complex and continually evolving with each new piece of research.

The Search for Genetic Links

I n 2010 researchers at Yale University announced that they had identified a gene that appeared to be a key contributor to the onset of depression. "This could be a primary cause, or at least a major contributing factor, to the signaling abnormalities that lead to depression,"[34] says Ronald S. Duman, professor of psychiatry and pharmacology at Yale and senior author of the study.

In the study, Duman's research team took brain tissue samples from 21 deceased people who had been diagnosed with depression. They also took tissue samples from 18 people who had not been diagnosed with depression. The researchers did whole genome scans on the samples. Then, they compared the results between the two groups. They discovered that one gene, called MKP-1, was twice as active in the depressed group as it was in the nondepressed group. "We chose to look at MKP-1 since it was the mostly highly abnormally regulated. We felt that it was possible that this gene could be very important and a potential trigger to depression,"[35] says Duman.

> **genome**
>
> All of the genetic information in an organism.

The research team then used rats to test their theory that MKP-1 was involved in depression. They found that when the MKP-1 gene was activated, the rats acted depressed when exposed to stress. When the gene was deleted, the rats were resistant to stress.

Based on the study's results, researchers are now searching for a way to block the MKP-1 gene as an alternate treatment for depression. "Depression used to be viewed as weakness not illness. Understanding the biochemistry and molecular and cellular changes demonstrates this is a biological illness that has to be treated and taken care of,"[36] says Duman.

What Are Genes?

Most scientists believe that one of the causes of mental illness lies in a person's genes. Every cell in a living organism has genes. Genes are pieces

of DNA that hold instructions that determine how an organism forms, what it looks like, and how it behaves in its environment. Genes are inherited, which means they are passed down from parents to children. Genes can be slightly different from person to person. These differences make each person unique.

Genes provide codes for the body to make proteins, which are the molecules that carry out most of the body's work, perform most life functions, and make up the majority of cellular structures.

mutations

Changes in genes.

Small changes, or mutations, in the DNA sequences of genes occur regularly. Most variations are harmless. Some variations, however, cause disease by altering the protein or the amount of protein produced.

Some diseases and disorders, such as cystic fibrosis, can be caused by the mutation of a single gene. Other disorders are caused by a combination of environmental factors and mutations in multiple genes. For example, several genes have been discovered that influence whether a person has a higher risk of breast cancer. Because of the multiple pieces, multifactor diseases are harder to study than single-gene disorders. Scientists believe that mental illnesses are the result of multiple gene mutations.

A Genetic Link to Mental Illness

Research has shown that people from families with a history of mental illness have a greater risk of developing a mental illness themselves. For example, if a person has a parent or sibling with major depression, he or she is one and a half to three times more likely to develop it.

Bipolar disease has an even stronger family connection. Fifty percent of people with bipolar disorder have a parent with a history of clinical depression. A child with one parent with bipolar disorder has a 25 percent greater chance of developing the disorder. If both parents have it, the child's risk increases to between 50 and 75 percent. These findings suggest a genetic link to mental illness.

However, scientists are still figuring out which genes are involved and how they influence mental illness. "Mental disorders are the most complex of all diseases. We're learning more about how genes can control the different biologic pathways in the brain, but more importantly, how that brain is wired to respond to environmental factors. We're at the

The Building Blocks of Genetic Research

Research has shown that a family history of mental illness increases the risk of developing the disease. For this reason, scientists are investigating possible hereditary, or genetic, links to mental illness. All genetic research begins from the same point: a basic understanding of chromosomes, genes, and DNA. Within each cell is a nucleus and within the nucleus are the chromosomes. Human beings have 23 pairs of chromosomes; these hold the genes that determine the characteristics of living things. Spooled within the chromosomes is the long, stringy DNA that makes up genes. Researchers are investigating the possibility that gene mutations might be passed through families and contribute to the development of mental illness.

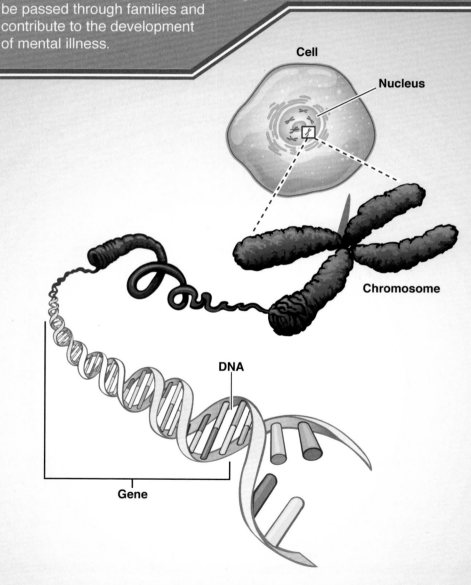

Cell

Nucleus

Chromosome

DNA

Gene

Source: National Institute of Mental Health, "The New Genetics." http://publications.nigms.nih.gov.

very primitive stages of knowledge,"[37] says Kathleen Ries Merikangas, a researcher in the NIMH Mood and Anxiety Disorders Program.

Because of the family connection, researchers have attempted to identify specific genes that may cause mental illness. To date, the answers have been slow to emerge because of the complexity involved in mental illness. Researchers believe that no single gene causes mental illness. Instead, they believe that mental illness is linked to a complex combination of genes and environmental factors such as stress. "We've known that genes play a significant role in the risk of these disorders. But until very recently, it's been difficult to impossible to identify genes that lead to these illnesses,"[38] says Jordan Smoller, director of the Psychiatric Genetics Program in Mood and Anxiety Disorders at Massachusetts General Hospital.

Twin Studies

To understand how genes influence mental illness, researchers sometimes conduct twin studies. Identical twins share the exact same genes, while fraternal twins share only 50 percent of their genes. If a mental illness is more common within identical twin pairs than fraternal pairs, researchers believe this means the illness has a genetic component.

In a twin study for ADHD, researchers found that a child with an identical twin with ADHD had a 75 percent chance of also having the disorder. Researchers studying bipolar disorder have also found a genetic link. If one identical twin has bipolar disorder, the other twin has a 60 to 80 percent chance of developing the disorder. Fraternal twins have only a 20 percent chance of developing the disorder if the other twin has it. These findings suggest that genes are a major factor in who develops ADHD and bipolar disorder. Yet, these studies also indicate that environmental influences affect who develops these disorders, because both identical twins did not develop the disorders in every case even though they shared the same genes.

Family Links: Bipolar and Schizophrenia

In 2009 researchers in Sweden announced that they had found evidence for a common genetic cause for bipolar disorder and schizophrenia. The two mental illnesses cause similar symptoms in patients. This led doctors to theorize that the two disorders shared a common genetic cause. To answer the question, the Swedish researchers analyzed three decades of data from 9 million Swedish families. They attempted to use the data to assess the risk for schizophrenia and bipolar disorder among biological and nonbiological relatives of patients with one or both of the disorders.

Their analysis showed that parents, siblings, or offspring of patients with either schizophrenia or bipolar disorder had an increased risk for developing both illnesses. People who had a sibling with schizophrenia were nine times more likely to develop schizophrenia and four times more likely to develop bipolar disorder than the general population. If a sibling had bipolar disorder, a person was eight times more likely to develop bipolar disorder and four times more likely to develop schizophrenia. Half siblings also had an increased risk of developing either disorder if their half sibling had either bipolar disorder or schizophrenia. Adopted children whose biological parent had either disorder also had a significant increase in risk of developing one of the mental illnesses.

> **hereditary**
>
> Passing from parent to offspring through the genes.

According to study researchers, the results suggest that schizophrenia and bipolar disorder are hereditary diseases and the same genes may be involved. "It is time that we rethink the way we view these disorders. And it is clear that we need more genetic studies to help us better understand this shared risk,"[39] says study coauthor Christina Hultman.

Identifying Genes

In order to understand the role of genes in mental illness, scientists first need to identify the genes within DNA that impact mental illness. To do this, scientists often start by looking for genetic markers or easily identifiable segments of DNA in family members with a history of a particular mental illness. If they find a pattern of markers inherited by people with the disease that are not found in relatives who are disease free, it may point to a section of DNA that is associated with the mental disorder. For example, if several family members have depression, scientists can analyze their DNA looking to find sections they all have in common. These common sections may be where the genes that influence depression are located.

Scientists then look more closely at these regions of DNA. They pull out specific genes to try to identify variations or mutations in the genes that may make a person more susceptible to developing a disorder. "If we can narrow our search to one part of the gene, then we can really focus

How Geneticists Find Disease Genes

Linkage analysis is the first step scientists take when trying to identify which genes cause a genetic disease. First, they collect blood samples from multiple generations of families where some members have the disease they are studying. The geneticists study the samples and follow the inheritance of parts of chromosomes from generation to generation. Then they look for similarities in the chromosomes for the family members affected by the disease.

For example, researchers might study the chromosomes of a great grandmother who has bipolar disorder. When they conduct a linkage analysis on her family's blood samples, they might discover that her relatives who also have bipolar disorder have a portion of Chromosome 2 that is exactly the same as hers. The affected relatives inherited this section from the great grandmother. In addition, family members who do not have bipolar disorder did not inherit that portion of Chromosome 2 from the great grandmother. With this information, scientists can say that a part of Chromosome 2 likely carries the gene that causes bipolar disorder in this family.

attention on that area to see if something there is linked to the disease,"[40] says Pamela Sklar, associate director of the Psychiatric and Neurodevelopmental Genetics Unit in the Center for Human Genetic Research at Massachusetts General Hospital.

In recent years, advances in gene identification technologies and DNA sequencing have allowed researchers to identify and study more genes and their relationship to mental illness. The ability to sequence whole genomes in multiple study participants has allowed researchers to study the differences between healthy people and those with mental illness. They hope that more full genome sequencing research efforts will help scientists understand the variations in genes and how they contribute to mental illness.

Searching for the Genetic Link to Autism

Autism spectrum disorders (ASDs) are complex mental illnesses. They are a group of developmental disabilities that can impair social and communication skills. People with ASDs may also exhibit restricted and repetitive behavior. ASDs affect each person in different ways. They can be very mild to severe.

Scientists believe that the symptoms of autism occur because information processing in the brain malfunctions. They suspect this occurs because of an alteration to nerve cells and how they connect and organize. While many scientists believe autism has a genetic component, the specific genes have not been identified.

In 2008 a consortium of autism researchers reported that they had conducted a complete genome scan of more than 3,000 children and families. Each family had at least one child with autism or a related disorder. The researchers discovered that a section on chromosome 16 that was either deleted or duplicated appeared to raise the children's risk for developing autism. "This has given us another piece of the puzzle of the genetics of autism. Autism is very complex, and we have only a few pieces in hand. We're trying to gain an understanding of the biological mechanisms underlying it. This is an opportunity to understand that,"[41] says study leader Mark Daly, a member of the Autism Consortium with the Center for Human Genetic Research at Massachusetts General Hospital in Boston.

consortium

An association, partnership, or union.

While they have identified an area of DNA to investigate, scientists still have more work to locate the specific genes associated with autism. The area under study has about 25 genes whose function is not clearly known yet. "We don't know from this study which of those genes is the critical one, or whether abnormalities in more than one of the genes are causing autism,"[42] says Christopher Walsh, chief of genetics at Children's Hospital Boston and a coauthor on the study. Researchers hope to go back and study the patients more carefully in an effort to understand how that section of chromosome 16 and its deletion or duplication affects brain function and autism.

In addition to chromosome 16, researchers studying autism have found more than a dozen genetic defects in other chromosomes that

Chromosome 16, seen in this colored scanning electron micrograph, might play a part in the development of autism. Researchers are trying to determine whether the deletion or duplication of a section of this chromosome increases the risk of autism.

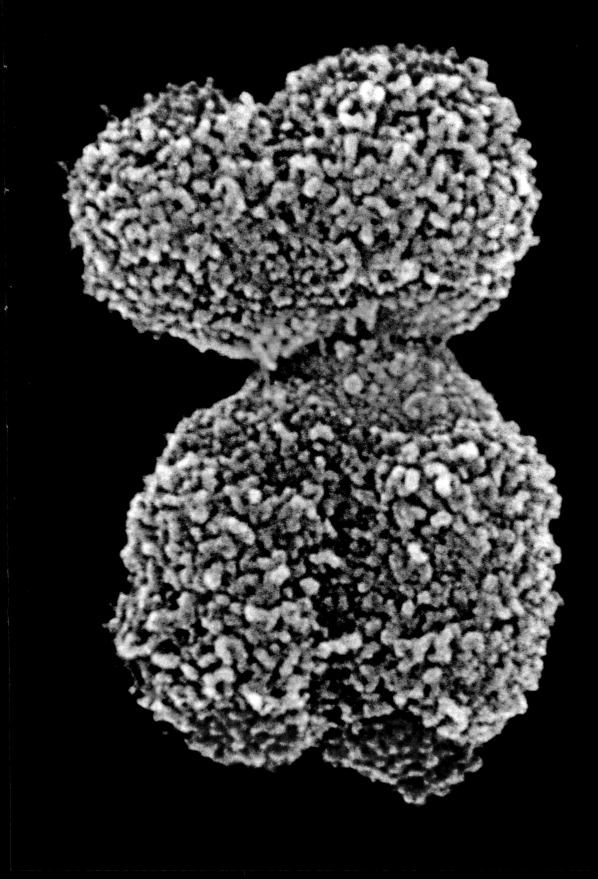

appear to be associated with autism spectrum disorders. Researchers from Children's Hospital Boston and members of the Boston-based Autism Consortium studied large families in the Middle East and Turkey for a genetic autism connection. They found five new genes that may be linked to autism. "While it might seem discouraging that it's a growing list of genes, we can be encouraged that a common pathway is emerging,"[43] says Walsh.

The researchers noted that while the identified genes may be in different locations on the 23 human chromosomes, each of the genes appeared to be involved in the learning process. These genes play a role in the physical and biochemical changes in the brain that occur when a person learns something new. "The implication of the study is that autism may be a result of molecular defects in the learning process,"[44] says Eric Morrow, a lead author on the study.

Breakthroughs in Schizophrenia and Bipolar Disorder

Until lately, most mental disorders have been largely defined by the behaviors that patients exhibit rather than the biological and genetic changes they cause. In recent years, scientists have made several breakthroughs studying how genes influence who develops a mental illness. "The discoveries we're witnessing now are the culmination of about 15 years of studying the genetic links to mental illness,"[45] says Smoller.

In the study of schizophrenia, researchers at many centers are working to identify the genes that influence the devastating mental disorder. Several gene variations that involved the deletion or duplication of large sections of DNA have been linked to an increased risk of schizophrenia. In a 2011 study, Jonathan Sebat, assistant professor of psychiatry and cellular and molecular medicine at the University of California at San Diego, and his team scanned the genomes of more than 8,200 patients with schizophrenia and 7,400 healthy control subjects. They scanned each study participant's genome for copy number variants (CNV), which are either duplications or deletions of genes. "We found very strong links to multiple sites in the genome. Some had been picked up in our earlier work, but we uncovered an important new finding—duplications at the tip of chromosome 7q were detected in individuals with schizophrenia at a rate that was 14 times higher than in healthy controls. These CNVs impact the *VIPR2* gene, which is important for brain development,"[46] says Sebat.

Sebat also says that each gene that researchers uncover helps to shed more light on the biology of schizophrenia. Although all patients with schizophrenia do not have this particular variant, it will help researchers learn more about the disease. "Just because only 1 in 300 patients has this mutation doesn't mean that only 1 in 300 patients has a problem with this signaling pathway. There may actually be a broader segment of schizophrenia patients who have something that is related to this, so uncovering this particular piece of the puzzle is actually quite important,"[47] he says.

> **predisposes**
>
> Makes susceptible beforehand.

In a large 2010 depression study, genetic researchers identified a duplicated area of DNA on chromosome 5 that predisposes people to depression. The duplicated gene has an important role in the development of nerve cells. "The copy number variations we discovered were exclusive to people with depression, and were located in a gene region important in signaling among brain cells. This finding extends work by other researchers suggesting that disruptions in neurotransmitter networks in the brain are an underlying cause of major depressive disorders,"[48] says study leader Hakon Hakonarson, director of the Center for Applied Genomics at The Children's Hospital of Philadelphia.

More Questions

Despite breakthroughs in the genetic study of mental illness, scientists admit that much more work needs to be done. Although some areas of DNA and mutations have been linked to mental illnesses, the vast majority of patients with the disorders do not have these large genetic mutations. Scientists need to work on identifying how variations in the sequence of genes may be associated with susceptibility and resistance to mental disorders. Scientists are working to learn how many more genes and what combinations of genes could underlie these diseases.

In addition, as sections of DNA are linked to mental illness, researchers will need to figure out how these genetic variations influence the way genes work and how the proteins they produce cause changes in brain structure, chemistry, and behavior. In addition, researchers are also studying how genes interact with behavior, experience, and environment to contribute to mental illness. According to the NIMH, "With the sequencing of the human genome, improved understanding of how genes are expressed, and new technologies to measure variation in the genome,

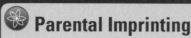

Parental Imprinting

Some diseases and disorders are inherited from a genetic mutation. Scientists are beginning to understand, however, that whether the mutated gene came from a patient's mother or father sometimes matters. This phenomenon is called parental imprinting, by which the gene inherited from one parent is always silenced or always expressed. For example, if a person inherits a mutation on chromosome 15 from his or her mother, that person will develop Angelman syndrome, a neurological disorder that causes intellectual and developmental delays, speech impairment, and jerky movements. If that person inherits the exact same chromosome 15 mutation from the father, however, it will result in a different disorder—Prader-Willi syndrome, a disease that causes an insatiable appetite and reduced muscle tone and mental ability.

In 2010 scientists discovered in mouse studies that parental imprinting plays a role for over 1,300 genes involved in shaping the brain's structure and function. Genes inherited from the father were more likely expressed in the hypothalamus. Genes from the mother were more likely expressed on the brain's cortex. Scientists believe that these findings show that the rules for gene expression in the brain may be more complex than ever thought.

we have an unprecedented opportunity to define how genes confer risk for the major mental disorders, potentially yielding new diagnostic and therapeutic targets."[49]

Genes and the Environment

As scientists study how genes influence mental illness, there is also a growing understanding in the scientific community that genetics and environmental factors sometimes act together to cause mental illness. "It is not a question of genes versus environment. It is a question of how genes interact with whatever the environmental factors might be. And that is probably true of all of the disorders that we call mental illness. There is going to be a genetic factor that gives you the risk. And it all depends on what happens in a person's lifetime,"[50] says Thomas R. Insel.

In one study in 2008, researchers at Emory University in Atlanta reported that they had found variations in a gene that regulated a stress hormone and appeared to give some protection from depression. In the study, participants who had the genetic variation and who also had a history of abuse experienced half the symptoms of depression as compared with participants who did not have the variation of the gene. This study supported findings from a previous 2003 study in New Zealand that found that people with a genetic variation of a gene that regulated the neurotransmitter serotonin were more likely to develop depression after experiencing an emotional trauma such as a job loss or death of a loved one. "When we study genes in conjunction with environmental challenges, we can better understand how diseases develop,"[51] says Mikhail V. Pletnikov, associate professor of psychiatry and behavioral sciences at the Johns Hopkins University School of Medicine.

Not a Complete Picture

In the past decade, scientists have made a number of significant breakthroughs in researching how genes affect mental illness. Yet mental illness is a complex disease, likely caused by a complicated interaction of multiple genes and environmental factors. Scientists are still discovering the gene variations that contribute to mental illness. Those that have been identified are often only a tiny piece of the puzzle. Yet scientists hope that genetic research will one day make it possible for doctors to build a more complete picture of a person's risk of developing a mental illness. They hope that genetic research will also lead to better diagnostic tools that could lead to earlier and more personalized interventions.

Even a person who carries the genetic mutations linked to mental illness is not certain to develop a disorder. To date, scientists have not identified any gene mutations that can predict with 100 percent accuracy whether a person will develop a mental illness. "Psychiatric illnesses are all about nature and nurture. Things like stress, adversity, and substance abuse factor into the equation; all are risk factors just like we're identifying the genes that are risk factors. Genes are not destiny,"[52] says Smoller.

Developing Treatments and Therapies for Mental Illness

At the beginning of ninth grade, Ashley began to struggle with feelings of unhappiness, even though she was a popular, straight-A student. She experienced panic attacks and could not concentrate. She also started thinking about hurting herself. "I just wasn't myself. I didn't want to live and felt worthless,"[53] says Ashley. She shared her feelings with her mother, who then took Ashley to the doctor. The doctor diagnosed Ashley with depression and anxiety and prescribed an antianxiety medication.

Despite the medication, Ashley's thoughts of hurting herself returned. She was hospitalized and prescribed an additional antidepressant medication. In spite of the changes, Ashley's new treatment did not work. A few days after returning home from the hospital, Ashley began to plan her suicide. Over the next year, doctors tried to control her mental illness by hospitalizing Ashley several times, and they prescribed a changing cocktail of medications. "I was frustrated. Already in two hospitals, discharged, and on medications, but I still didn't feel like myself,"[54] she says. Eventually, Ashley swallowed an overdose of pills, which landed her in the emergency room. After being stabilized and hospitalized again, she eventually learned coping skills to help manage her depression. Today at age 19, she manages her illness with weekly therapy and medication.

For many patients like Ashley, treatment for mental illness can be difficult and frustrating. Many current treatments are not successful for all patients. Patients may suffer through years of their illness before they find the right treatment plan that minimizes their symptoms and allows them to function normally in their lives. "We need to get recurrent affective disorders treated with better and more effective preventative treatments. If somebody has too many episodes, it's not good for them as a person and it's not good for their brains, either. . . . Treating mental illness earlier is critical,"[55] says Robert Post, adjunct professor at the George Washington School of Medicine in Washington, DC.

Over the years, medical advances have improved the treatment of mental illness. Most current mental illness treatment falls into two categories: somatic or psychotherapeutic. Somatic treatments include drug therapy and electroconvulsive therapy. Psychotherapeutic treatments include different types of talk or behavioral therapy. Understanding the causes of mental illness helps doctors successfully tailor somatic or psychotherapeutic treatment to each disorder and each patient.

> **somatic**
>
> Relating to the human body as distinct from the mind.

Treating Mental Illness

A number of medications are widely used to treat mental illnesses. Medications do not cure mental illnesses. Instead, they treat symptoms and make people feel better so they can function. Some of the first medications to treat depression were developed in the late 1950s and early 1960s. In the late 1980s, as scientists learned more about brain function and the role of neurotransmitters in depression, new medications called selective serotonin reuptake inhibitors (SSRIs) were developed. These medications prevent neurons from removing serotonin from the brain's synapses.

While SSRIs have become popular as antidepressants, other medications have also been developed to treat mental illnesses. For bipolar patients, mood stabilizers help smooth out mood swings. The most commonly prescribed mood stabilizer is lithium. It works by controlling the amount of the neurotransmitter glutamate in the brain. Too-high glutamate levels can trigger a manic episode, while too-low levels can cause a depressive episode. For patients with bipolar disorder, a doctor may prescribe antidepressants to treat depressive episodes, medication for anxiety or agitation, or antipsychotic medications.

Although medications have helped many mental illness patients manage their illness, they are far from perfect. Many medications take at least a month to start working. In addition, patients often experience unpleasant side effects such as nausea, weight gain, and sleeplessness. Many patients decide to stop taking medication without their doctor's approval. Some stop because they think the medicine is not working. Others stop because they cannot tolerate the side effects. Regardless of the reason, patients who stop their medication too soon risk a return of their mental illness symptoms.

When severe cases of mental illness do not respond well to other treatments, doctors might recommend electroconvulsive therapy (ECT). ECT is especially effective for those who are extremely depressed, suicidal, or experiencing severe mania. During ECT, electrodes deliver electrical impulses to locations on the head. While the patient does not feel the impulses, the electrical stimulation causes a 30-second seizure in the brain. Doctors believe ECT affects the chemical balance of the brain's neurotransmitters. "It is the most effective and rapidly acting treatment for severe depression,"[56] says Sarah Lisanby, a professor of clinical psychiatry at Columbia University Medical Center.

electrodes

Conductors through which pulses of electricity are applied to the scalp during some mental illness treatments.

Psychotherapy Treatments

Since the 1970s, the use of psychosocial therapy, sometimes called talk or cognitive therapy, to treat mental illness has increased significantly. Talk therapy can occur in individual, group, or family sessions. During a session, the patient talks to a mental health professional about his or her feelings and problems and learns ways of dealing with them.

The most common types of talk therapy are cognitive-behavioral therapy (CBT) and interpersonal therapy (IPT). CBT is based on the idea that people's thoughts influence their feelings and behaviors. Negative thoughts about a situation will lead to negative feelings and behaviors. Therefore, CBT tries to change how people think about a situation and teach ways to respond more positively and feel better. A 2009 study in the *Journal of the American Medical Association* reported that CBT works well for adolescents with depression. After six months, teens assigned to CBT sessions were less likely to become depressed than teens assigned to traditional talk therapy. IPT focuses on a patient's relationships with others. The therapist helps the patient understand how interacting with other people affects their moods. During IPT, the patient learns strategies to develop healthier relationships with family and friends.

As with medications, not all individuals respond to psychosocial therapy. Only a minority achieve full remission. In addition, most treat-

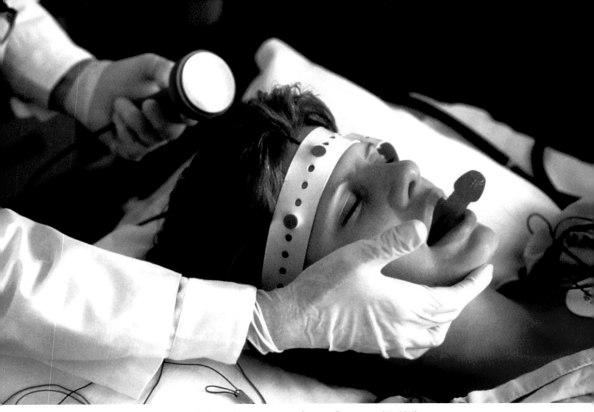

A patient is prepared for electroconvulsive therapy (ECT), sometimes used to treat severe cases of depression or mania. During this procedure an electrical current passes through the brain, causing a brief seizure. Doctors believe ECT restores the chemical balance of neurotransmitters in the brain.

ment research on mental illness has suggested that treatment with a combination of medication and psychotherapy is often more effective than either treatment alone.

Search for More Effective Treatment

Scientists are using advances in knowledge about the brain and emotions to revisit and redesign existing treatments to make them more effective and prevent patient relapses. They also use studies of brain chemistry and how medications act on the brain to help them develop new medical and psychotherapy treatments.

Recognizing the need for more effective treatments, the NIMH launched two large research studies concentrating on the treatment of depression and bipolar disorder. In the depression study Sequenced Treatment Alternatives to Relieve Depression, or STAR*D, researchers

studied more than 4,000 patients between 1998 and 2005. They record-
ed and analyzed the effectiveness of different treatments after the patient
did not respond to initial treatment with an antidepressant. The study
found that while treatment-resistant depression could be treated in some
cases, a patient's odds of beating depression decreased as additional treatment strategies were needed. "This new STAR*D
report reminds us that treating depression remains
a formidable challenge. While roughly two-thirds
of patients report remission, many subsequently
relapse. We need new treatments that are rapid,
enduring, and individualized to facilitate recovery,"[57] says Insel.

remission

A period when
symptoms of a disease
lessen or disappear.

In the bipolar study Systematic Treatment Enhancement Program
for Bipolar Disorder (STEP-BD), researchers examined the role of bipolar medications and compared several types of psychotherapy to identify
the most effective treatments. "STEP-BD is helping us identify the best
tools—both medications and psychosocial treatments—that patients
and their clinicians can use to battle the symptoms of this illness,"[58] says
Insel. In the study, researchers found that intensive psychotherapy was
more effective than brief therapy for patients already taking medications
to treat bipolar disorder. While psychotherapy is regularly used to treat
bipolar illness, its effectiveness had previously been unclear. "We know
that medication is an important component in the treatment of bipolar
illness. These new results suggest that adding specific, targeted psychotherapy to medication may help give patients a better shot at lasting
recovery,"[59] says Elias A. Zerhouni, former director of the National Institutes of Health.

Researching New Medications

Brain studies are helping scientists develop new medications to treat
mental illness more efficiently and effectively. One way to research new
medications is to map the brain circuits that are not functioning normally in mental illness. In depression studies, scientists can monitor the
level of function in selected brain areas while a study subject performs a
mental task. This monitoring can also be done before and after antidepressant treatment to compare the baseline activity in a patient's brain
with the activity after treatment.

Clinical Trials

Researchers use clinical trials to test new medications, therapies, or other treatments, usually with the aim of finding a better way to prevent, screen for, diagnose, or treat a disease. Such trials can also be used for comparing a new treatment against a currently available treatment, to see which works better.

Researchers follow a protocol or action plan when conducting the clinical trial. The protocol tells them what to do and how to do it. It makes sure that researchers in different locations perform the trial in the same way. In the United States, an independent committee of doctors, statisticians, and members of the community approve and monitor a clinical trial protocol. They make sure that the risks to study participants are small.

Each clinical trial also has rules about who can participate. A clinical trial may ask for volunteers with a specific disease or mental illness. It may also ask for healthy volunteers. During the trial, researchers collect data on the study volunteers' health for a set period. The researchers then send that data to the clinical trial's sponsor, who analyzes the data using statistical tests.

Clinical trials are performed in several phases. At first researchers conduct small trials with small groups of patients. If positive results are found, researchers may then conduct larger trials with many more volunteers. In the United States, clinical trials are usually required before a new drug or device can be used on patients.

Knowing how medications work can help scientists develop targeted and potent medications that work more quickly to relieve symptoms. Existing antidepressant drugs influence the functioning of certain neurotransmitters in the brain, in particular serotonin and norepinephrine. For depressive illnesses, these commonly prescribed antidepressant medications fail in up to 40 percent of patients. They also take several weeks to begin working. Scientists believe this happens because the medications trigger slow, adaptive changes in the brain cells, or neurons. In addition, understanding the action of medications can also help scientists understand why certain medications produce side effects. This can lead to the development of more tolerable medications and treatments.

Ron Duman of Yale University is researching how an experimental drug called ketamine appears to be a fast-acting treatment for major depression. NIMH scientists have found that 70 percent of treatment-resistant major depressive and bipolar patients improved dramatically within a day after receiving just one dose of ketamine. Rat studies have shown that ketamine likely works by rapidly stimulating connections between brain cells or neurons. Duman's team is studying the brain to understand why that happens. "The studies that we've conducted have demonstrated that ketamine is able to rapidly activate a component of the neuron that's responsible for new protein synthesis and in particular synthesis of proteins that are important for new synapses and we believe it's that formation of new synapses and the connections between neurons that's important for the rapid action of ketamine,"[60] says Duman.

Despite the promise it shows in experimental studies, ketamine has side effects that some doctors believe make it impractical as a long-term treatment. Nevertheless, future research on how ketamine affects the brain and brain chemistry could provide critical insights that may lead to the development of other fast-acting medications for mental illness. "This may be a key to developing medications that eliminate the weeks or months patients have to wait for antidepressant treatments to kick in,"[61] says lead researcher Carlos A. Zarate Jr. of the NIMH Mood and Anxiety Disorders Program.

Improving Treatment Outcomes

Some scientists are studying how treatment choices affect patients' chances of successfully managing their mental illness. Current medication and psychotherapy treatments usually take weeks to show improvement in a patient's symptoms. In fact, current depression guidelines recommend that patients remain on a treatment for eight to twelve weeks before switching to another medication or type of therapy.

A 2010 NIMH-funded study, however, found that a patient's early response to a prescribed treatment predicted whether he or she would eventually achieve remission of symptoms. The study followed teens with hard-to-treat depression who had not responded to a first course of medication. The teens were assigned to a second course of treatment, either a different medication or a new medication plus CBT therapy.

Pierre Blier Advancing Knowledge of Antidepressants

Pierre Blier is a professor at the University of Ottawa, Department of Psychiatry and Cellular/Molecular Medicines. For the past 25 years, Blier has been involved in studying antidepressant treatments. He has focused on trying to learn how antidepressant medications work and how to make them work better and faster. As part of his research, Blier has studied the effects of medications and has searched for new cellular targets for treatment. He has also worked on developing new treatments. As part of his research, Blier concentrated on the neurotransmitter serotonin, which is thought to be a key component through which antidepressant medications work. Blier has also been studying the neurotransmitter norepinephrine and how it affects antidepressant response.

A world-renowned scientist, Blier has received several awards for his groundbreaking research in mental illness. He is also a member of the Brain and Behavior Foundation's Scientific Council, a group of leading mental health researchers that advises the foundation on research grants.

Researchers discovered that nearly 40 percent of those who completed 24 weeks of treatment achieved remission, regardless of the treatment course to which they had been assigned. However, those who achieved remission were more likely to have responded to the treatment within the first six weeks as compared with those who did not achieve remission at all. "These results suggest that early treatment decisions are probably the most crucial to the recovery of teens with hard-to-treat depression,"[62] says Insel. The study suggests that waiting twelve weeks to change a treatment may be too long. More research, however, is needed to clarify when is the best time to abandon one treatment and switch to another.

Behavioral Science

Some researchers study cognition, emotion, and behavior in mental illness. They seek to understand why certain behaviors occur in specific situations. They also develop tools to measure, shape, and change behavior. Psychotherapy is one of the tools that behavioral scientists have developed to shape and change behavior for mental illness patients. Psychotherapy works by changing the way the brain functions and forming

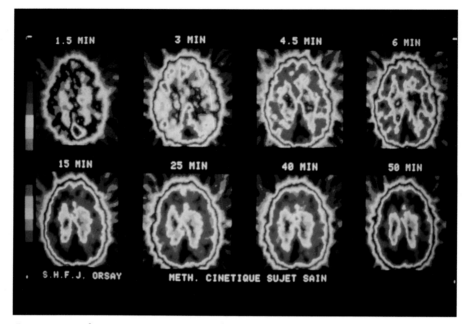

Protein synthesis is an important function of the brain; improper protein synthesis may be a factor in major depression. A radioactive tracer (red) shows active protein synthesis in this series of scans of a normal human brain. Scientists are studying drugs that can activate protein synthesis in the brain.

new connections between nerve cells in the brain, similar to the learning process.

Research on psychotherapy and how it affects mental illness is an important part of mental illness research. Scientists study different therapy treatments and how each affects patients. They also study how therapy works when used alone or in combination with other treatment options such as medication.

In 2008 researchers analyzed dozens of studies on cognitive-behavioral therapy. They concluded that CBT was an effective treatment for reducing symptoms related to depression, anxiety, and post-traumatic stress disorder in teens and adolescents. "The good news is there is substantial research showing the effectiveness of group or individual cognitive-behavioral therapy in treating children and teens experiencing the psychological effects of trauma. We hope these findings will encourage clinicians to use the therapies that are shown to be effective,"[63] says Robert Hahn, study coauthor and researcher at the Centers for Disease Control and Prevention.

Knowing that CBT helped patients who already had depression, NIMH-funded researchers in 2009 studied whether a preventative program of CBT would be effective at helping at-risk teens avoid depression. Researchers assigned 316 at-risk teens to either a CBT program or a usual care program. Teens in the CBT program received eight weekly 90-minute group CBT sessions. Therapists helped them learn to restructure dysfunctional thinking patterns and practice problem-solving skills. After the first eight weeks, participants followed up with six monthly sessions in which they reviewed skills and learned new techniques. Teens assigned to usual care participated in mental health or other health care services in their communities.

The researchers reported that CBT was more effective in preventing the onset of depressive symptoms in the at-risk teens. Teens in the CBT program experienced depression 21.4 percent of the time as compared with 32.7 percent for teens in the usual care program. In addition, the teens in the CBT program who did experience depression symptoms reported lower levels of symptoms as compared with teens in the usual care program. The study's results show that preventive treatment programs for mental illness can be effectively delivered. "For every 9 adolescents who received the cognitive intervention, we would expect to prevent one from developing a depressive episode,"[64] says study researcher Judy Garber of Vanderbilt University.

In a 2010 study of bipolar patients, researchers from the University of Melbourne in Australia found that psychosocial interventions such as cognitive-behavioral therapy could help people with bipolar disorder from relapsing after they have been stabilized with medication. Lead investigator David Castle divided 72 participants into two groups. Over a 12-week period, one group received medication. The second group received medication and followed a structured group psychosocial therapy plan. During the nine months after the study period, the second group experienced fewer bipolar relapses (4) as compared with the first group (15).

relapse

The return of a disease or illness after a partial recovery from it.

Adapting Existing Treatment

Other mental illness researchers are investigating how to adapt current treatments for new uses. One adaptation, called dialectical behavior therapy (DBT), evolved when Marsha Linehan, a psychology professor and director of the Behavioral Research and Therapy Clinics at the University of Washington in Seattle, observed shortcomings in applying cognitive-behavioral therapy to adult women who had borderline personality disorder (BPD). People with this personality disorder often have low self-esteem and have a hard time regulating their emotions. Patients with severe cases may try to harm themselves or attempt suicide.

At first, Linehan investigated whether cognitive-behavioral therapy could help her borderline personality disorder patients. She found, however, that many of her patients resisted CBT's focus on change. Many dropped out of treatment. Those who remained often became angry or distressed when the therapist talked about their past in order to help them make changes in their present lives. Because of the difficulty in implementing CBT with these patients, Linehan looked to adapt the therapy to make it work for BPD patients.

Linehan and her team introduced dialectics, a process of balancing acceptance and change, into treatment for BPD patients. The resulting dialectical behavior therapy helps patients identify thoughts, beliefs, and assumptions that make their lives challenging and then learn different ways of thinking and reacting. The idea is "to validate the person's emotional reactions, to say, 'I understand how you feel,' to pay attention, not to the situation, but to the emotion behind it,"[65] says Linehan. Using DBT, Linehan's patients exhibited less suicidal behavior, were more likely to remain in treatment, and rated themselves more successful at changing and controlling their emotions.

The success of DBT in treating patients with borderline personality disorder has led to its use for other types of mental illness. Researchers are investigating the effectiveness of DBT for cases of substance abuse, patients with mental illness and developmental delays, and bipolar disorder.

Improving Treatment

Expanding knowledge about the brain and the factors that influence mental illness is aiding researchers in the development of new medications and therapies and in finding ways to use existing treatments more effectively.

Despite the progress that has been made in recent years, researchers are working toward improved mental illness treatments. Traditionally, treatment or intervention research has focused on reducing the symptoms of mental illness. Yet scientists recognize that reducing symptoms does not cure the disease. In some cases, existing treatments do not work, or side effects impair a patient's ability to function in everyday life. So mental health researchers will continue to search for treatments that help every patient recover from mental illness. According to the NIMH Strategic Plan, "We will improve existing approaches and devise new ones for the prevention, treatment, and cure of mental illness, allowing those who may suffer from these disorders to live full and productive lives."[66]

The Future of Mental Illness Research

In October 2010, Rules-Based Medicine, Inc., a biomarker testing laboratory, announced that it had developed a commercial blood test to aid in confirming the diagnosis of recent-onset schizophrenia. "There is a certain amount of denial when a child is diagnosed with schizophrenia. You wish that your child did not have that. It is a good test to convince parents or even the patient to stay on medication, as opposed to just subjective opinion,"[67] says Michael Spain, chief medical officer at Rules-Based Medicine.

The blood test, called VeriPsych, measures biomarkers, which are proteins or pieces of genetic material found in the bloodstream. These biomarkers can indicate that a condition or a disease is present. To diagnose a patient with schizophrenia, scientists compare the blood of the patient with the blood of a person known to have the mental disorder.

At first, researchers analyzed 200 biomarker candidates to assess their connection to schizophrenia. They discovered 51 biomarkers with links to schizophrenia. In a later study, researchers tested the ability of a blood test to identify the 51 biomarkers for schizophrenia. Spain led a study that collected blood samples from 577 patients with schizophrenia. His research team compared the biomarkers in those blood samples with those of 229 people without schizophrenia. They found that the blood test was accurate at diagnosing 83 percent of patients. "Schizophrenia is a complicated and challenging disease, yet current diagnostic approaches continue to be based on patient interviews and a subjective assessment of clinical symptoms. We expect VeriPsych to be used as an aid to this current process, and we hope it will provide the psychiatrist

> ### biomarker
>
> An objective biological measure such as a protein, antibody, or DNA sequence that is used to assess health or diagnose disease.

with additional confidence in their evaluation, as well as speed up the process,"[68] says Sabine Bahn, director of the Cambridge Centre for Neuropsychiatric Research and one of the scientists who worked on development of the blood test.

Bridging the Gap

Today, diseases such as heart disease and diabetes can be prevented and managed from the earliest stages because scientists understand how these diseases develop and how to identify risk factors. Mental illness researchers hope that insights from neuroscience, genetics, and behavioral science will help them one day identify and treat mental illness in the same way. "Once we are better able to predict risk for psychosis and have homed in on the biological changes associated with the emergence of psychosis, our chances for preventative intervention will be greatly

Greater understanding of the risk factors for mental illness might one day allow doctors to prevent its onset. Advances in various fields of study as well as in techniques such as brain imaging (pictured) are leading to that day.

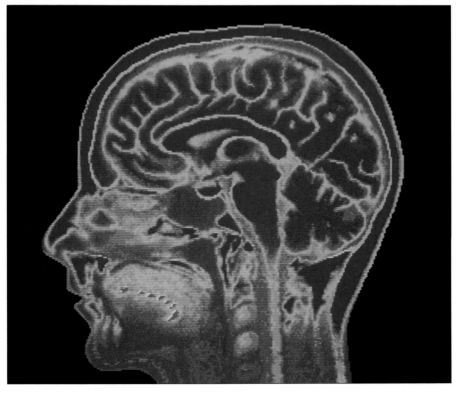

Nancy C. Andreasen, Neuroscientist

Nancy C. Andreasen is an award-winning neuroscientist and psychiatrist at the University of Iowa. She is well known for her investigations of mental illness and the biological processes of the brain. For the past two decades, she has studied the brain and long-term changes in healthy and diseased brains. A trailblazer in many areas, Andreasen was the first to use twin populations to study genetic and environmental interactions. She was also one of the first to use powerful techniques such as magnetic resonance imaging (MRI) to study the brain in mental illness.

Today, Andreasen's research uses a variety of neuroimaging techniques for three-dimensional reconstruction, statistical analysis, and automated measurements. In recognition of her research, Andreasen received a National Medal of Science in 2000, one of the United States' highest awards in science. She is the author of more than 200 scientific articles and 10 books.

improved. Prevention is the ultimate goal,"[69] says Elaine Walker, professor of psychology at Emory University in Georgia.

Advances in neuroscience, genetics, and behavioral science are helping scientists identify how the brain works and what goes wrong in mental illness. Understanding how and why brain circuits malfunction in mental illness may allow scientists to diagnose patients earlier. Brain imaging, genetic testing, and diagnostic blood testing may eventually be able to identify a problem or a patient's elevated risk. Then, doctors can tailor effective treatment to an individual's specific case.

Biomarkers

One of the greatest challenges for the future of mental illness research is finding a better way to diagnose, prevent, and treat mental illness. For many illnesses like diabetes and cardiovascular disease, doctors routinely use biomarkers to help predict risk and diagnose and manage the disease. Biomarkers are components in the bloodstream that can indicate health status. In heart patients, cardiac enzymes are biomarkers that confirm a heart attack. Lipid profiles and the presence of C-reactive protein in the blood help predict a patient's risk of heart disease. Other common biomarkers include cholesterol, estrogen, and glucose.

Yet for major mental disorders, few biomarkers have been developed to aid in the management of these illnesses. Currently the traditional assessment and diagnosis of mental illness is based on a patient's self-reporting of symptoms or a doctor or therapist's evaluation of a patient's symptoms.

As scientists learn more about how mental illness affects brain activity patterns, chemicals, and structures, they hope to identify biomarkers that will help them better diagnose a variety of mental illnesses. According to the NIMH, "The identification, characterization, and validation of biomarkers/biosignatures for the major mental disorders would facilitate accurate prediction of disease risk, course, and therapeutic responses and ultimately lead to knowledge-based treatment and preventive strategies."[70]

In addition to the blood test for schizophrenia, other researchers are working to develop biomarkers that will help them identify depression and bipolar disorder. In 2011 Japanese researchers announced that they had developed a simple blood test for depression by measuring the concentration of phosphoric acid in the blood. Patients with depression had a lower concentration of phosphoric acid The new test could improve early detection of depression if performed during regular doctor checkups. "The findings will make it easier for an objective, biological diagnosis of depressive patients. We believe that the use of such a test will make it possible to diagnose patients efficiently at the primary care stage,"[71] says Yoshiaki Ohashi, a board director and chief security officer at the study sponsor medical research group Human Metabolome Technologies.

Personalized Care

Many times patients respond differently to the same treatments. Finding the right treatment for a patient is often a haphazard process in which their doctors try different options until they find the best one. "Questions remain as to how best to optimize these treatments and why these treatments work for some and not others. We still do not know who will respond to a specific treatment. Clinicians often must resort to trial and error before finding a treatment regimen that works, often subjecting patients to weeks of ineffective treatment or adverse side effects in the process. For individuals

> **regimen**
>
> A regulated course, as of diet, exercise, or medication, intended to preserve or restore health or to attain some result.

and families contending with a life-threatening illness, the delay can be torturous,"[72] says Thomas Insel.

Scientists believe that a better understanding of the brain will lead to more targeted and curative treatments in the future. An emerging medical practice called personalized medicine may soon change the way doctors treat mental illnesses. Personalized medicine will use a patient's unique genetic makeup to identify the optimal medication or treatment for them. This approach has the potential to help doctors determine in advance what therapies will work for a patient with the least disruptive side effects.

For schizophrenia, the potential of personalized medicine is enormous. Choosing the correct medication for schizophrenia patients is frequently a challenge. Current studies show that less than one in three patients will have an improvement in symptoms with the first drug prescribed. Currently, poor response to medication and unpleasant side effects lead to approximately 50 percent of patients stopping their medication within six months.

In 2010, researchers at SureGene LLC and the Medco Research Institute launched a study to understand if genetic biomarkers for schizophrenia can help predict how patients will respond to different antipsychotic medications. The proposed clinical trial will collect DNA samples from study participants. "A study of this nature has the potential to show that understanding a patient's genetic risk with the help of a diagnostic test can improve antipsychotic drug selection, efficacy, safety, and compliance. [It] could help provide evidence supporting the development of a genetic test that may assist physicians to make a personalized treatment decision for patients with these serious diseases,"[73] says Felix Frueh, Medco's vice president of Personalized Medicine Research and Development.

> **efficacy**
>
> The quality of being successful in producing an intended result; effectiveness.

Researchers hope that advances in personalized medicine will change treatment for schizophrenia and other serious mental illnesses. Knowing how a patient might respond to a certain medication will help doctors overcome previous challenges.

Gene Therapy

In addition to using genes to guide treatment choices, scientists are also working on ways to use gene therapy to treat mental illness in the

The Promise of Gene Therapy

Gene therapy might someday provide a way to treat mental illness. Still in the experimental stages, gene therapy involves the insertion of a normal, healthy gene into a target cell where it will replace an abnormal or mutated gene that is causing illness. A vector—usually a genetically altered virus—is used to infect the target cell and then deliver the therapeutic gene (and its normal, healthy DNA) to that cell. This process generates a protein product that restores the target cell to a normal state. All of this occurs deep inside the cell. Within the cell is a nucleus. Within the nucleus are 23 pairs of chromosomes. The chromosomes contain the genes, which are made up of DNA. These are the elements that make gene therapy possible.

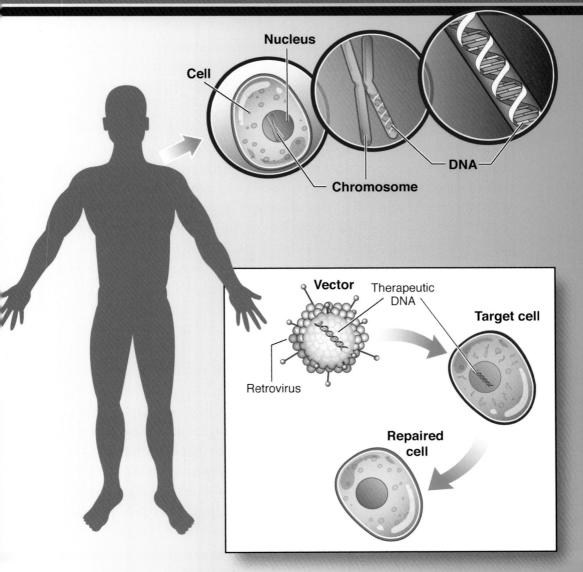

Source: Food and Drug Administration, "Fundamentals of Gene Therapy," August 14, 2000. www.fda.gov.

future. Gene therapy, or using genes to treat or prevent disease, is currently an experimental treatment. One day, however, it might allow doctors to treat a disorder by inserting a gene into a patient's cells to replace a mutated gene with a healthy copy of the gene. Doctors may be able to inactivate an improperly functioning gene or introduce a missing gene into a patient to help fight a disease.

Researchers at the Weill Cornell Medical College in New York City have been studying gene therapy and depression. In a 2010 study led by Michael Kaplitt, the team identified an area of the brain where a lack of a key protein may be a factor in depression. They found that depressed people had lower than normal levels of a protein called p11. Scientists believe that p11 helps brain cells detect serotonin, a neurotransmitter that regulates mood. "We believe that low levels of p11 may be one of the causes of depression in at least some patients. If we can restore it to normal levels, we can potentially reverse the process,"[74] says Kaplitt.

> **inactivate**
>
> To make something stop acting or working.

To test the connection of p11 and depression, Kaplitt's team disabled the function of the gene that produces p11 in mice. They used a virus that blocked the gene's expression. Without the p11 protein, the mice exhibited depressed behavior. Then the researchers injected the mice with a virus that carried a working copy of the p11 gene back into the nucleus accumbens, a brain area that is critical to the feelings of reward and pleasure. They discovered that cells in the brain area began producing the protein and the mice stopped exhibiting depressed behavior. Kaplitt and his team hope that their findings in mice will lead to a human trial that uses gene therapy to treat depression.

New Line of Study: Epigenomics

Although genes are an important component of understanding mental illness, scientists have become increasingly aware that a person's experiences and environment also play a critical role in brain development and mental illness. A new line of research called epigenomics is focused on studying how events and environment affect gene and brain function.

Genes direct the production of the body's proteins. They also carry compounds that regulate when, where, or how much protein is made. Genes can switch between active phases when they direct protein production and silent phases when no protein is produced. Epigenetics is the study of the pattern that results when a gene switches between active and silent phases. Studies suggest that epigenetic markers develop as an animal adapts to its environment. These markers can affect behavior and may influence mental illness.

The NIH is sponsoring several studies to investigate the relationship between genes, epigenetic markers, and behavior. While epigenetics focuses on individual genes, epigenomics is the study of epigenetic changes across many genes in a cell or organism. Scientists hope that epigenomic research will help them understand patterns of gene function. They also hope to identify targets for treatments that could

⚛ Treating Bipolar Disorder with Magnetic Waves

A new high-tech, noninvasive therapy has been developed to treat patients with bipolar disorder. Known as transcranial magnetic stimulation or TMS, the treatment sends a series of electromagnetic pulses to the brain's left prefrontal cortex, which regulates mood. The pulses generate an electric current in the brain. This stimulates neurons to increase their production of the brain chemicals serotonin, dopamine, and norepinephrine, which are known to improve mood. A recent study published in the journal *Brain Stimulation* found TMS to be an effective, long-term treatment for depression.

For John O'Sullivan, TMS brought hope. He had struggled with bipolar disorder since he was a teen. Different combinations of psychotherapy and medication never seemed to work for long. For a three-week period, O'Sullivan received TMS treatment five days a week in half hour sessions. He did not need to be sedated and could receive the treatment on an outpatient basis in his psychiatrist's office. So far, O'Sullivan has been impressed with the results. While medication would take six to eight weeks before he knew if it would work, he says he felt dramatically better a short time after TMS. "The results have been what I would call surprisingly good. From my experience going back to my teenage years, I've never been as optimistic about life as I am now after TMS. I feel like a million bucks. I feel great. It's a pretty big change."

Quoted in Loyola University Health System, "Magnets Used to Treat Patients with Severe Depression," *ScienceDaily*, October 19, 2010. www.sciencedaily.com.

increase or decrease the activity of affected genes. "A lot of the model systems we have studied suggest that epigenetic modifications impact behavior, and also that those effects can be reversed,"[75] says Thomas Lehner, chief of the genomics research branch of the National Institute of Mental Health.

In a 2010 study, researchers at Johns Hopkins University School of Medicine studied how chronic stress affects genes. Scientists have known that stress can increase the risk of depression. Yet they have been unable to pinpoint how stressful life events affect the biology of depression.

James Potash, an associate professor at Johns Hopkins, and his team believe that epigenetics might be the answer. To test if stress could leave epigenetic markers on the genes related to depression, Potash and his team put corticosterone in the drinking water of mice for four weeks. Corticosterone is a version of cortisol, a hormone produced in stressful situations. A control group of mice drank plain water. At the end of four weeks, researchers discovered that the mice that drank the corticosterone water showed anxious characteristics during behavior tests. The research team found an increase in a protein produced by a gene called Fkbp5. In humans, the same gene is linked to mood disorders. The scientists then studied the mouse DNA for epigenetic markers on Fkbp5. They found significantly fewer methyl groups attached to the gene as compared to the DNA for the mice that drank the plain water. The researchers suspect that the number of methyl groups could be a potential epigenetic marker, showing how the same gene expresses in different ways. The differences in the epigenetic markers continued for several weeks, suggesting a long-term change. "This gets at the mechanism through which we think epigenetics is important,"[76] says Potash, who directs Johns Hopkins's Mood Disorders Research Programs.

Potash says that doctors may someday be able to look for these epigenetic markers in a patient's blood. They could use the tests to predict or diagnose mental illness. They may also be able to develop medication that targets epigenetic markers to treat depression and other mental illnesses.

Defining the Trajectory of Mental Illness

As mental illnesses are increasingly classified as brain disorders, scientists are also beginning to think of these disorders as chronic conditions that change over a patient's lifetime. Symptoms may begin in childhood and vary through each phase of life. Patients with other neurodegenerative diseases such as Parkinson's or Huntington's disease show behavioral and cognitive symptoms years after the disease begins damaging the brain. Scientists are working to define mental illnesses in a similar way. In this manner, mental illnesses would be seen as disorders that progress along a course that begins with risk, and then evolves into early symptoms, later develops into full-blown disorders, and then moves into cycles of remission and relapse.

neurodegenerative

Progressive loss of structure or function of neurons.

NIMH researchers believe that understanding the trajectory of mental illnesses will help them better identify the best times to prevent symptoms and disease. Intervening and treating early in the disease timeline, doctors could dramatically improve the chances of a patient's life not being disrupted by a mental disorder.

To understand the path of mental illness, scientists are studying how the brain develops normally from infancy through childhood, adulthood, and old age. They are looking at periods of vulnerability for the emergence of risk, onset of symptoms, remission, or relapse. To help in this understanding, recent brain studies have mapped the pattern of brain development in healthy youth and compared it with those with mental illness. In one brain-mapping study, researchers found a difference in the development of brains between healthy individuals and schizophrenia patients. Although some loss of neurons and connections is normal as the brain matures into adulthood, adolescents identified with childhood onset schizophrenia show four times the normal rate of brain loss in the front of the brain.

In a large 2008 neuroimaging study, researchers compared the brain scans of more than 200 children with ADHD with another 200 without the disorder. They found that both groups of children experienced similar patterns of brain development. However, in the ADHD brains, the maturation of the prefrontal cortex was delayed by approximately three years. This area of the brain controls thinking, attention, and planning. "The sequence in which the different parts of the brain mature is very similar in the two groups. I think this is probably quite good evidence that a large component of ADHD is due to delay in brain development. If you show that ADHD is due to a delay in brain development, perhaps we should be looking at factors that disturb the timing of how the brain

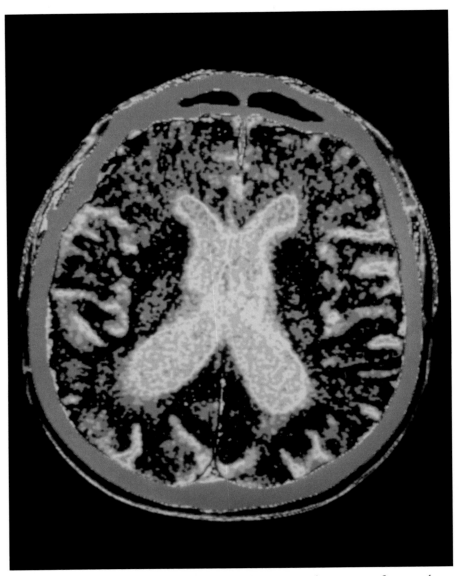

Doctors might be able to treat mental illness at earlier stages if researchers can identify symptoms that appear and change over time. This is what happens with illnesses such as Parkinson's disease. A colored brain scan shows the enlarged fluid-filled ventricles that are characteristic of a person with Parkinson's disease.

develops,"[77] says lead study author Philip Shaw, a researcher at the National Institute of Mental Health. For example, Shaw's team is looking at how the genes that sculpt the cortex of the brain turn on and off, to see whether they provide further clues about what is delaying brain development in ADHD.

A Long Road Ahead

Although many breakthroughs have occurred in mental illness research in recent years, scientists acknowledge that there is still a lot about the brain and mental illness that they simply do not understand. According to Bruce Cohen, professor of psychiatry at Harvard Medical School, understanding mental illness is "going to take a lot more work than we hoped. We're going to have to study tens of thousands of people, and there are so many factors. At this point it's a matter of time, money, and work—but it's a very hopeful future."[78]

Source Notes

Introduction: Changing Lives

1. Quoted in Timothy Johnson, "Woman Battles Schizophrenia for Normal Life," The Boston Channel.com, February 22, 2005. www.thebostonchannel.com.

2. Quoted in Johnson, "Woman Battles Schizophrenia for Normal Life."

3. Quoted in Johnson, "Woman Battles Schizophrenia for Normal Life."

4. Thomas R. Insel, "Director's Message," National Institute of Mental Health Strategic Plan. www.nimh.nih.gov.

5. Quoted in *The Science of Mental Illness*, video, Minds on the Edge. www.mindsontheedge.org.

6. Quoted in *The Science of Mental Illness*.

Chapter One: What Is Mental Illness?

7. Quoted in WHDH-TV.com, "Who Is Loughner? Those Who Knew Him Speak Out," January 11, 2011. www1.whdh.com.

8. Quoted in Kate Pickert and John Cloud, "If You Think Someone Is Mentally Ill: Loughner's Six Warning Signs," *Time,* January 11, 2011. www.time.com.

9. Shonda Schilling, "Family Profiles: Shonda, Age 42, Major Depression, with Husband Curt and Children," Families for Depression Awareness. www.familyaware.org.

10. Quoted in Maiken Scott, "Documentary Explores Challenges of Living with Mental Illness," WHYY.org, July 15, 2010. http://whyy.org.

11. Quoted in Jeffrey Kluger, "Young and Bipolar," *Time*, August 19, 2002. www.time.com.

12. Quoted in Tamar Morad, "Genes and the Mind," *Mass General Magazine*, Summer 2009. www.massgeneralmag.org.

13. Quoted in Charles W. Schmidt, "Environmental Connections: A Deeper Look into Mental Illness," *Environmental Health Perspectives*, August 1, 2007. http://ehp03.niehs.nih.gov.

14. Quoted in Emily Anthes, "Getting Ahead of Trouble: Early Detection of Mental Illness May Keep It from Spiraling Out of Control," *Boston Globe*, September 6, 2010. www.boston.com.

15. Quoted in Anthes, "Getting Ahead of Trouble."

16. Quoted in Cassandra Spratling, "Minorities Lag in Mental Health Treatment, but Some Are Working to Change That," *Detroit Free Press*, July 16, 2011. www.freep.com.

17. Quoted in National Institute of Mental Health, "Mental Illness Exacts Heavy Toll, Beginning in Youth," press release, June 6, 2005. www.nimh.nih.gov.

18. Quoted in Spratling, "Minorities Lag in Mental Health Treatment."

19. Quoted in Courtney Reyers, "What Are They Thinking? Research, Diagnosis and Mental Illness," *Advocate*, October 2010. www.nami.org.

20. Quoted in National Institute of Mental Health, "NIMH's Dr. Mortimer Mishkin to be Awarded National Medal of Science," November 12, 2010. www.nimh.nih.gov.

Chapter Two: Looking Deep Inside the Brain

21. Quoted in Live Science, "Depression Linked to Brain Thinning," March 26, 2009. www.livescience.com.

22. Thomas R. Insel, "Faulty Circuits," *Scientific American*, April 2010. p. 44.

23. Quoted in Rick Nauert, "Brain Scans May Predict Schizophrenia," PsychCentral.com, December 25, 2010. http://psychcentral.com.

24. Quoted in Nneka McGuire, "State Institute Pioneers Depression Finding with PET Scan Research," *Columbia Spectator*, April 29, 2009. www.columbiaspectator.com.

25. Quoted in McGuire, "State Institute Pioneers Depression Finding with PET Scan Research."

26. Quoted in University of Illinois at Chicago, "Brain Imaging Identifies Differences in Childhood Bipolar Disorder, ADHD," *ScienceDaily*, January 19, 2011. www.sciencedaily.com.

27. Quoted in University of Illinois at Chicago, "Brain Imaging Identifies Differences in Childhood Bipolar Disorder, ADHD."

28. Quoted in *Depression: Out of the Shadows*, video, PBS, 2008.

29. Insel, "Faulty Circuits," p. 47.

30. Quoted in Carolyn Y. Johnson, "On a Quest to Map the Brain's Hidden Territory," *Boston Globe*, October 11, 2010. http://articles.boston.com.

31. Quoted in National Institutes of Health, "NIH Launches the Human Connectome Project to Unravel the Brain's Connections," July 16, 2009. www.nimh.nih.gov.

32. Quoted in Johnson, "On a Quest to Map the Brain's Hidden Territory."

33. Insel, "Faulty Circuits," p. 47.

Chapter Three: The Search for Genetic Links

34. Quoted in Yale Office of Public Affairs & Communications, "Yale University Researchers Find Key Genetic Trigger of Depression," Yale University, October 17, 2010. http://opac.yale.edu.

35. Quoted in Jennifer Nadelmann, "Gene Illuminates the Origins of Depression," *Yale Daily News*, October 20, 2010. www.yaledailynews.com.

36. Quoted in Nadelmann, "Gene Illuminates the Origins of Depression."

37. Quoted in David Gutierrez, "Psych Setback: New Study Demolishes Genetic Link to Depression," *Natural News*, November 4, 2009. www.naturalnews.com.

38. Quoted in Tamar Morad, "Genes and the Mind," *Mass General Magazine*, Summer 2009. www.massgeneralmag.org.

39. Quoted in Salynn Boyles, "Schizophrenia, Bipolar Disorder: Gene Link?," WebMD, January 15, 2009. www.webmd.com.

40. Quoted in Charles Schmidt, "The Scarlet Gene," *Proto Magazine—Massachussetts General Hospital*, Fall 2005. http://protomag.com.

41. Quoted in Amanda Gardner, "Chromosome Abnormalities Raise Risk for Autism," *U.S. News and World Report*, January 9, 2008. http://health.usnews.com.

42. Quoted in Children's Hospital Boston, "New Chromosome Abnormality Linked to Autism Spectrum Disorders," January 9, 2008. www.childrenshospital.org.

43. Quoted in Claudia Wallis, "New Clues to Autism's Cause," *Time,* July 10, 2008. www.time.com.

44. Quoted in Morad, "Genes and the Mind."

45. Quoted in Morad, "Genes and the Mind."

46. Quoted in Fran Lowry, "Schizophrenia Gene Mutation Discovered," Medscape, February 3, 2011. www.medscape.com.

47. Quoted in Lowry, "Schizophrenia Gene Mutation Discovered."

48. Quoted in *ScienceDaily,* "Gene Duplication Detected in Depression; Finding Points to Disruptions in Brain Signaling Networks," December 1, 2010. www.sciencedaily.com.

49. National Institute of Mental Health, "The National Institutes of Health Strategic Plan." www.nimh.nih.gov.

50. Quoted in Julie Steenhuysen and Ben Hirschler, "Nature and Nurture Play Role in Mental Illness," Reuters.com, February 4, 2008. www.reuters.com.

51. Quoted in Traci Pedersen, "Gene Mutation in Schizophrenia Linked to Mood, Anxiety Disorders," PsychCentral.com, December 7, 2010. http://psychcentral.com.

52. Quoted in Morad, "Genes and the Mind."

Chapter Four: Developing Treatments and Therapies for Mental Illness

53. Quoted in Families for Depression Awareness, "Ashley, Age 19, with Clinical Depression and Anxiety, with Mom Lucy." www.familyaware.org.

54. Quoted in Families for Depression Awareness, "Ashley, Age 19, with Clinical Depression and Anxiety, with Mom Lucy."

55. Quoted in Courtney Reyers, "A Lifetime of Research: Robert Post, M.D., on Bipolar Disorder and the Future of Treatment," *NAMI Advocate,* Winter 2011, p. 21.

56. Quoted in Sarah Baldauf, "If the Gloom Won't Lift," *U.S. News & World Report,* December 2009.

57. Quoted in National Institute of Mental Health, "Odds of Beating Depression Diminish as Additional Strategies Are Needed," November 1, 2006. www.nimh.nih.gov.

58. Quoted in National Institute of Mental Health, "Intensive Psychotherapy More Effective than Brief Therapy for Treating Bipolar Depression," April 2, 2007. www.nimh.nih.gov.

59. Quoted in National Institute of Mental Health, "Intensive Psychotherapy More Effective than Brief Therapy for Treating Bipolar Depression."

60. Ron Duman, "NIMH Radio: Dr. Ron Duman of Yale University Talks About Ketamine Research and Treatment for Major Depression," September 9, 2010. www.nimh.nih.gov.

61. Quoted in National Institute of Mental Health, "Experimental Medication Kicks Depression in Hours Instead of Weeks," August 7, 2006. www.nimh.nih.gov.

62. Quoted in National Institute of Mental Health, "Early Treatment Decisions Crucial for Teens with Treatment-Resistant Depression," May 26, 2010. www.nimh.nih.gov.

63. Quoted in Centers for Disease Control and Prevention, "Cognitive Behavior Therapy Effective for Treating Trauma Symptoms in Children and Teens," September 9, 2008. www.cdc.gov.

64. Quoted in National Institute of Mental Health, "Re-shaping Negative Thoughts Shields At-Risk Teens from Depression," June 9, 2009. www.nimh.nih.gov.

65. Quoted in Jane Brody, "An Emotional Hair Trigger, Often Misread," *New York Times*, June 15, 2009. www.nytimes.com.

66. National Institute of Mental Health, "The National Institutes of Health Strategic Plan," p. 18.

Chapter Five: The Future of Mental Illness Research

67. Quoted in Natasha Allen, "It's in the Blood: New Hope for Detecting Schizophrenia," My Health News Daily, October 13, 2010. www.myhealthnewsdaily.com.

68. Quoted in PhysOrg.com, "New Blood-Test to Aid in Schizophrenia Diagnosis," July 1, 2010. www.physorg.com.

69. Quoted in Courtney Reyers, "What Are They Thinking?," *NAMI Advocate,* October 2010.

70. National Institute of Mental Health, "Research on Biomarkers for Mental Illness," February 13, 2009. www.nimh.nih.gov.

71. Quoted in Danielle Demetriou, "Near Instant Blood Test to Diagnose Depression," *Daily Telegraph* (London), May 24, 2011. www.telegraph.co.uk.

72. Thomas R. Insel, "Taking Clinical Research to the Next Level," National Institute of Mental Health, August 30, 2010. www.nimh.nih.gov.

73. Personalized Medicine Coalition, "SureGene and the Medco Research Institute Enter a Collaboration to Evaluate the Ability of Genetic Biomarkers to Enhance Drug Selection for Serious Mental Illnesses," August 24, 2010. www.personalizedmedicinecoalition.org.

74. Quoted in Laura Sanders, "Gene Therapy for Depression," *U.S. News and World Report*, October 21, 2010. www.usnews.com.

75. Quoted in Benedict Carey, "Genes as Mirrors of Life Experiences," *New York Times*, November 8, 2010. www.nytimes.com.

76. Quoted in Traci Pedersen, "Chronic Stress Leaves Mark on Depression, Bipolar Genes," Psychcentral, September 17, 2010. http://psychcentral.com.

77. Quoted in Marlene Busko, "In ADHD, Brain Maturation Follows Normal Pattern but Is Delayed," Medscape, May 7, 2008. www.medscape.com.

78. Quoted in Reyers, "What Are They Thinking?"

Facts About Mental Illness

Prevalence of Mental Illness

- According to the National Alliance on Mental Illness (NAMI), one out of four American families has a relative who has a mental illness.

- Major depressive disorder is the leading cause of disability among Americans aged 15 to 44.

- The World Health Organization estimates that depression will be the number one cause of disability in the developed and developing worlds by 2030.

- According to NAMI, about 2.4 million Americans, or about 1.1 percent of the US population aged 18 and older, live with schizophrenia.

- According to NAMI, bipolar disorder affects 5.7 million American adults, or about 2.6 percent of the US population aged 18 and older, in a given year.

- Mental illness typically strikes young people between the ages of 16 and 25, according to NAMI.

- The median age of onset for mood disorders is 30 years old.

- According to NAMI, 1 in 10 American children has a serious mental or emotional disorder.

- Women experience depression at twice the rate of men.

Risk Factors in Mental Illness

- Children of depressed parents are two to three times more likely to develop depression than are children who do not have a family history of the disorder.

- Thirty-three percent of bipolar patients have at least one bipolar parent.

- Some 20 percent of adolescents with major depression develop bipolar disorder within five years of the onset of depression.

- Mental illnesses thought to have the strongest genetic components include autism, bipolar disorder, schizophrenia, and ADHD.

- Stressful or traumatic events such as the death of a close family member or friend, parent's mental illness, divorce, economic hardship, abuse, and neglect can increase an individual's risk for mental illness.

Cost of Mental Illness

- In the United States, the annual indirect cost of mental illness is estimated to be approximately $79 billion, with most of that relating to lost productivity, as reported by NAMI.

- Mental disorders are as disabling as cancer or heart disease in terms of premature death and lost productivity.

- Individuals living with serious mental illness have an increased risk of having chronic medical conditions, such as heart disease and type 2 diabetes.

- According to NAMI, more than 90 percent of people who die by suicide have a diagnosable mental disorder.

- Over 50 percent of students with a mental disorder aged 14 and older drop out of high school—the highest dropout rate of any disability group, as reported by NAMI.

- Eighty to 90 percent of people who live with a serious mental illness are unemployed, as reported by the 2008 PBS program, *Depression: Out of the Shadows*.

Treatment of Mental Illness

- According to NAMI, fewer than one-third of adults and one-half of children with a diagnosable mental disorder receive mental health services in a given year.

- According to a study by researchers at Harvard University, two-thirds of inmates from local, state, and federal correctional institutions were off treatment for a mental illness at the time of their arrest.

- Ten million people in the United States are taking prescription antidepressants.

- A common medication, lithium, is effective in controlling mania in 60 percent of individuals with bipolar disorder.

- A study by researchers at several universities, including the Harvard School of Public Health, reported that the level of care received differed by race and ethnic group with African Americans (40 percent) and Mexican Americans (34 percent) least likely to receive depression treatment.

- A depressive episode, left untreated, can last six months or, chronically, for years.

- Untreated depression is the number one risk for suicide among youth.

Related Organizations

American Academy of Child and Adolescent Psychiatry

3615 Wisconsin Ave. NW
Washington, DC 20016
phone: (202) 966-7300
fax: (202) 966-2891
website: www.aacap.org

The academy is a national professional medical association dedicated to treating and improving the quality of life for children, adolescents, and families affected by mental, behavioral, or developmental disorders.

American Foundation for Suicide Prevention (AFSP)

120 Wall St., 22nd Floor
New York, NY 10005
phone: (888) 333-2377
fax: (212) 363-6237
e-mail: inquiry@afsp.org
website: www.afsp.org

The AFSP is the leading national not-for-profit organization dedicated to understanding and preventing suicide through research, education, and advocacy and to reaching out to people with mental disorders and those impacted by suicide. The foundation funds scientific research, offers educational programs, promotes legislation, and provides resources for people at risk for and survivors of suicide.

American Psychiatric Association

1000 Wilson Blvd., Suite 1825
Arlington, VA 22209
phone: (888) 357-7924
e-mail: apa@psych.org
website: www.psych.org

The American Psychiatric Association has over 38,000 US and international member-physicians working together to ensure humane care and effective treatment for all persons with mental disorders. It publishes many books and journals, including the widely read *American Journal of Psychiatry*.

American Psychological Association

750 First St. NE
Washington, DC 20002-4242
phone: (800) 374-2721
e-mail: public.affairs@apa.org
website: www.apa.org

The American Psychological Association represents more than 148,000 American psychologists, who are professionals who study and treat problems of human behavior. Its website features information about psychology topics, including mood disorders and links to many publications.

Association for Behavioral and Cognitive Therapies

305 Seventh Ave., 16th Floor
New York, NY 10001
phone: (212) 647-1890
fax: (212) 647-1865
website: www.abct.org

This association represents therapists who provide cognitive-behavioral therapy for people who suffer from many types of mental illnesses, including mood disorders. The association's website features fact sheets on mental illnesses, including depression and bipolar disorders.

The Brain and Behavior Research Foundation

60 Cutter Mill Rd., Suite 404
Great Neck, NY 11021
phone: (516) 829-0091
fax: (516) 487-6930
e-mail: info@bbrfoundation.org
website: www.narsad.org

The Brain and Behavior Research Foundation (formerly NARSAD, the National Alliance for Research on Schizophrenia and Depression) is committed to alleviating the suffering of mental illness by awarding grants that will lead to advances and breakthroughs in scientific research.

Depression and Bipolar Support Alliance
730 N. Franklin St., Suite 501
Chicago, IL 60654-7225
phone: (800) 826-3632
fax: (312) 642-7243
e-mail: info@dbsalliance.org
website: www.dbsalliance.org

The Depression and Bipolar Support Alliances has more than 400 community-based chapters that provide support for people with mood disorders and their families. The alliance also provides educational materials to schools, the media, and other interested groups. It also lobbies in Washington for laws that support mental health education and research.

Mental Health America
2000 N. Beauregard St., 6th Floor
Alexandria, VA 22311
phone: (800) 969-6642
fax: (703) 684-5968
website: www.smha.org

Mental Health America is an advocacy group for people with mental illnesses and their families. Its website features many resources, including fact sheets on mood disorders, finding support groups, and how to take action to support research and funding for mental illnesses.

National Alliance on Mental Illness (NAMI)
Colonial Place Three
2107 Wilson Blvd., Suite 300
Arlington, VA 22201-3042
phone: (703) 524-7600
fax: (703) 524-9094
 website: www.nami.org

The National Alliance on Mental Illness is an advocacy group for people with mental illnesses and includes local chapters in every state. The alliance offers education programs and services for individuals, family members, health care providers, and the public. NAMI also serves as a voice for Americans with mental illness in Washington, DC, and state capitals across the country.

National Institute of Mental Health

6001 Executive Blvd.
Bethesda, MD 20892-9663
phone: (866) 615-6464
e-mail: nimhinfo@nih.gov
website: www.nimh.nih.gov

The National Institute of Mental Health is the federal government's chief funding agency for mental health research in America. The institute's website provides fact sheets and information about mental illness, including mood disorders, and the latest science news and research on these illnesses.

For Further Research

Books

Terri Cheney, *Manic: A Memoir*. New York: William Morrow, 2008.

Russ Federman and J. Anderson Thomson, *Facing Bipolar: The Young Adult's Guide to Dealing with Bipolar Disorder*. Oakland, CA: New Harbinger, 2010.

Marya Hornbacher, *Madness: A Bipolar Life*. Boston: Houghton Mifflin, 2008.

Chelsea Swigget, *Rae: My True Story of Fear, Anxiety, and Social Phobia*. Deerfield Beach, FL: HCI Teens, 2010.

Hannah Westberg, *Hannah: My True Story of Drugs, Cutting, and Mental Illness*. Deerfield Beach, FL: HCI Teens, 2010.

Robert Whitaker, *Anatomy of an Epidemic: Magic Bullets, Psychiatric Drugs, and the Astonishing Rise of Mental Illness in America*. New York: Crown, 2010.

Periodicals

Thomas R. Insel, "Faulty Circuits," *Scientific American*, April 2010.

Brendan McLean, "Genes and Mental Illness: What's the Connection?," *NAMI Advocate*, Winter 2011.

Courtney Reyers, "A Lifetime of Research: Robert Post, M.D., on Bipolar Disorder and the Future of Treatment," *NAMI Advocate*, Winter 2011.

Websites

Making Sense of Research: Developing Critical Appraisal Skills (www.globalhealth.org/assets/publications/making_sense.pdf). This free report from the Global Health Council gives readers tips to assess clinical research in order to make more-informed decisions. It also offers useful questions to ask when examining the validity and rigor of a study, definitions of key terms, and tips for sources of further information.

National Institute of Mental Health: Health Topics (www.nimh.nih .gov/health/index.shtml). This page on the National Institute of Mental Health website has information on many types of mental illness. Resources include signs and symptoms, how to find help, treatment options, and related information links.

The National Institute of Mental Health Strategic Plan (www.nimh .nih.gov/about/strategic-planning-reports/index.shtml). This 2008 report details the NIMH's five-year strategic plan and areas of focus for mental health research.

On Being a Scientist: A Guide to Responsible Conduct in Research (www.nap.edu/openbook.php?record_id=12192&page=R1). This is a free, downloadable book from the National Academy of Sciences Committee on Science, Engineering, and Public Policy. The 2009 edition provides a clear explanation of the responsible conduct of scientific research. Chapters on treatment of data, mistakes and negligence, the scientists' role in society, and other topics offer invaluable insight for student researchers.

Understanding Mental Illness (www.uth.tmc.edu/uth_orgs/hcpc/men tal_illnesses.htm). The University of Texas Harris County Psychiatric Center's website offers information about types of mental illnesses, causes, signs and symptoms, myths, living with mental illness, treatments, and how friends and family can cope.

Index

Note: Boldface page numbers indicate illustrations.

INDEX

Picture Credits

Cover: iStockphoto.com

Maury Aaseng: 28, 42, 69

AP Images: 15

CNRI/Science Photo Library: 60

Dr. David Furness, Keele University/Science Photo Library: 23

GJLP/Science Photo Library: 74

Mehau Kulyk/Science Photo Library: 65

Will McIntyre/Science Photo Library: 55

Pasieka/Science Photo Library: 11, 31

Geoff Tompkinson/Science Photo Library: 35

Science Photo Library: 47

Thinkstock/iStockphoto.com: 8, 9 (top)

Thinkstock/Hemera: 9 (bottom)

About the Author

Carla Mooney is the author of many books for young adults and children. She lives in Pittsburgh, Pennsylvania, with her husband and three children.